HOW REAL ESTATE AGENTS TURN COLD CALLS INTO CLIENTS

REVERSE SELLING

reverseselling.com

BRANDON MULRENIN

© 2021 Brandon Mulrenin. All rights reserved.

No part of this book may be used or reproduced by any means, graphic, electronic, or mechanical, including photocopying, recording, taping, or by any information storage retrieval system without the written permission of the publisher except in the case of brief quotations embodied in critical articles and reviews.

The advice and strategies found in the book may not be suitable for all situations. Neither author nor publisher will be held responsible for the results of advice taken herein. Publisher and author are not responsible for any loss of profit, including but not limited to special, consequential, personal or other damages. For permission requests, write to support@reverseselling.com.

Reverse Selling: How Real Estate Agents Can Turn Cold Calls Into Clients / Brandon Mulrenin, — 1st ed.
ISBN 978-1-7374001-0-3

www.reverseselling.com

CONTENTS

	About the Author	v
	Acknowledgments	vii
	Introduction	ix
Chapter 1	The Reverse Selling Paradigm	11
Chapter 2	The Truth About Prospecting	13
Chapter 3	The Prospecting Millionaire Mindset	25
Chapter 4	The 23 Rules of Reverse Selling	33
Chapter 5	Reverse Selling Skills in Action	49
Chapter 6	Why Face-to-Face Meetings Change Everything	73
Chapter 7	Lead Generation	81
Chapter 8	The Prospecting Plan of Action	101
Chapter 9	The Fortune is Made in the Follow-Up	111
Chapter 10	Listing Agent Playbook	117

About the Author

Brandon Mulrenin is the creator of the Reverse Selling Method and the CEO of ReverseSelling.com and Brookstone Realtors. Brandon believes that being a salesperson should be something people are proud of. He believes that old, high-pressure selling is a thing of the past, and for salespeople to earn the respect back from society, they must first serve their clients before they try to sell them anything.

For more than 15 years, Brandon has been on the front lines of sales, leading salespeople, and sales leaders all over the country. Brandon is quickly becoming one of the most influential leaders in the sales training space. Brandon has coached thousands of real estate agents and salespeople and has helped them to achieve their highest goals by teaching them how to effectively sell and increase their productivity as a salesperson.

To learn more about coaching with Brandon, please visit ReverseSellling.com.

FOLLOW BRANDON MULRENIN

YouTube - Youtube.com/Brandon Mulrenin

Instagram - @BrandonMulrenin

Acknowledgments

Writing this book has been on my "to do" list for years and without the wonderful people who helped me get this book done, it would most likely still be sitting on my "to do" list. First, I'd like to thank my brother, Ryan Mulrenin, for helping me get clear on the concepts I've been teaching for years but have never been able to put into words—thank you! I want to thank my mother, Marlene Mulrenin, for her passion for the details. She's like my secret weapon when it comes to making a finished product.

I also want to thank my right hand in business, Jennifer Frye. Jennifer has been by my side throughout all my business ventures and the same goes for this book. She spent hours going through each concept to make sure I explained everything so it was easy to read and digestible. To my graphic designer, Caitlin Carroll, thank you! She has skillfully turned the cover of this book into reality and is my go-to for artistic vision in all of my businesses. I would also like to thank my editor for this book, Melody Marler. Hearing her words of encouragement helped to push me to finish this book and get it out to the world. Her expertise in this process is hard to describe in words and my team and I are forever grateful.

Finally, I'd like to thank my wife Amy and our three daughters, Vaughn, Vella and Vaira. Your unwavering love and support to complete this book and support in all my business ventures has facilitated accomplishing my goals, and has given me the ability to keep dreaming bigger.

Introduction

When you think of a salesperson, what comes to mind? Be honest. The unfortunate reality is that people believe salespeople cannot be trusted. In fact, research shows 97% of all consumers don't trust salespeople. And make no mistake, as a real estate agent you are, in fact, a salesperson. But don't take my word for it. Pull out your real estate license and read what it says. You'll find it says, "Real Estate Salesperson License."

It's important to understand why salespeople have this stigma. Studies have revealed the negatives, such as salespeople talking too much and not listening, lack of understanding of the prospects' actual desired outcome, and using high-pressure tactics. But most of all, the number one reason why most people don't trust salespeople is the salesperson's bias toward making a sale.

True or not, most people in a buying situation believe that the salesperson is biased toward "making the sale," whether it makes sense for the consumer to proceed or not. "Never trust a salesperson" has become one of the most common memes passed down through the generations, and this has created a paradigm in which salespeople and consumers are at odds with each other, making it more and more difficult for each to meet their mutual goals and objectives.

This is the core of the issue for salespeople like you and I. Working in sales weighs heavily on our moral conscience because, like everyone else, we too grew up believing that "salespeople are evil." And yet here we are—salespeople. This is the internal battle that eats away at so many of us on a daily basis and causes us to say things to ourselves like, "I won't make prospecting phone calls because if I do, I'm no different than the salespeople I was taught not to trust!"

So you're probably thinking, "How do I become the kind of salesperson that 3% of the general public actually does trust?" This book will help you do just that.

After you understand how to apply the Reverse Selling Method taught in this book, you'll have prospects easily agreeing to meet with you. It will become normal to hear prospects tell you how different your approach is and how much they appreciate your call. Yes! You heard that right, you will have prospects who are complete strangers actually thank you for calling them, whereas most of your prospecting experience has probably resulted in the prospect reaming you out, or worse yet, hanging up on you!

This book will change your mindset and what it means to be a salesperson. More importantly, this book will teach you the tactics, strategies, and methodologies that will change how the prospect responds and has the potential to change their perception of salespeople altogether.

While other real estate agents continue to use high-pressure tactics and argue with prospects over the phone, you'll learn how to make prospecting easy and something you look forward to doing.

You'll find it effortless to make prospecting calls and take listings, whereas before, just hearing the word "prospecting" most likely made you feel a little sick.

Introduction

In this book, I'll show you how to apply the Reverse Selling Method as a real estate agent. For years, I took the advice of many of the real estate "gurus" (you know the famous ones on YouTube) who suggested using high pressure to persuade prospects, and to overcome objections with authority by pushing the prospect to move forward. This style of selling no longer is effective with today's consumer. I will teach you what I personally do in my real estate business that has helped me to sell over 100 homes a year and to build one of the fastest growing independent real estate brokerages in the country.

Not only has the Reverse Selling Method helped me, I've now taught thousands of other real estate agents all over the world this exact same system. It's a system that, if mastered, has the potential to help you to go from where you are today to selling 50, 60, 70, even 100-plus homes a year! Even if you're a brand new agent, reading the concepts in this book will act as an outline for you to structure your business in becoming a top producing real estate agent. So let's get to work!

1 | The Reverse Selling Paradigm

There's a reason why 97% of the population doesn't trust salespeople. Until recently, selling was taught to be a process of using high-pressure tactics and strategies to convince a prospect to buy—convince being the key word. Salespeople from around the world have been taught to close the sale using any means necessary. Eventually, decades of fancy tactics and strategies, as well as hard-pitch closing techniques from salespeople, began to lose their effectiveness. This is where much of the world's resistance to salespeople originated and also why salespeople today must either adapt or be left behind. To make matters worse, Hollywood has amplified society's distrust for salespeople for years, with movies like "Glengarry, Glen Ross," "Boiler Room," and "Wolf of Wall Street" starring Leonardo DiCaprio. These movies, although great entertainment, further solidify the bias society has for salespeople and deepens the belief that salespeople cannot be trusted.

The majority of salespeople, however, want to use the product or service they sell to genuinely help people. This is often an uphill battle, thanks to the millions of salespeople and sales trainers before us who have contributed to society's deeply rooted hatred for the sales profession. So you continue to find yourself in situation after situation where your authentic willingness to help the prospect is blinded by the prospect's unapologetic bias. It's situations like this that lead to more negative self-talk, telling your subconscious mind that "selling is evil," leaving you to live with doubt that you've chosen the wrong profession.

What if there was a way of selling—a way of communicating—that altered the prospect's belief that you genuinely cared about helping them achieve their desired outcome, regardless of whether a sale was made? The good news—there is. We call it Reverse Selling.

Reverse Selling is a process in which a salesperson seeks to understand the prospect's true desired outcome versus traditional selling, which is a process where the salesperson tries to convince the prospect to buy. The Reverse Selling Method will teach you how to use the Socratic method in combination with neurolinguistic programming (NLP) to help the prospect feel safe to share their true desired outcome without the threat of being "sold." When it's done correctly, the Reverse Selling Method will help position you as the prospect's obvious choice without you ever having to convince them of it. You'll learn how to effectively sell without coming across as "salesy." The goal is to have the prospect decide on their own that doing business with you is the best decision through a process of self-discovery you strategically guide them through by asking Socratic-style questions.

2 | The Truth About Prospecting

"Get fit, get healthy, and live forever, all without exercise and eating whatever you want." It's marketing messages like these that are finally raising red flags and reinforcing the old adage, "If it's too good to be true, it probably is."

But not for real estate agents. For some reason, when we enter the real estate business, all common sense goes out the window. Marketers are screaming from the mountaintop, "You don't have to prospect, cold calling is dead," and it's exactly what we want to hear. These companies promise to let us off the hook by selling their new gadget or technology that will cause us to reach the success of our dreams, all without ever having to do the hard work of prospecting or talking to people. I know, it's crazy. But we buy it every day; these companies profit billions of dollars every year by targeting the weak. "Easy" is the world's greatest marketing strategy and we buy it, knowing it's too good to be true and knowing we're buying from someone who has never succeeded in the real estate business themselves.

In the world of real estate sales, there are low-producing agents, average producers selling six to eight homes a year, and top producers who are responsible for 80% of the sales. Agents in the top 20% prospect consistently, without excuses and without exception, while the bottom 80% chases shiny objects. You don't have to take my word for it—go meet with any top producer in any company, in any market around the world and they will all tell you the same thing: Prospecting and lead generation is the most important factor in determining whether you will be successful or not.

WHAT IS PROSPECTING?

Prospecting is not cold calling (more on that later). Prospecting is the simple act of proactively seeking out new business. Although some try to overcomplicate it, it's no mystery why 87% of all real estate agents end up failing in their first year. It's not because of the market, the company they are with, their broker, their manager, bad leads, the time of year, not knowing what to do—it's none of those. Real estate agents fail simply due to an empty sales pipeline. Why is their pipeline empty? You guessed it: They fail to prospect consistently.

WHY REAL ESTATE AGENTS DON'T PROSPECT

As I mentioned in the introduction, most untrained real estate agents are in a constant state of moral dilemma about being in sales. They want to help people, but at the same time, they can't bring themselves to accept the fact that to succeed in real estate sales, they must be willing to interrupt prospects daily. If you think for one second that you can sit back and wait for prospects to call you, you're wrong. If that was the case, the failure rate in real estate would be almost insignificant. But that's not the case—you and I both know this is not how it works. If you're going to win, you're going to have to play offense and proactively contact your prospects, knowing damn well they are not sitting around waiting for you to call.

In my research, I found four main reasons why real estate agents don't prospect.

1. Fear of Rejection and Embarrassment

For many, the fear of rejection is too overwhelming to handle. Therefore, they avoid the activity of prospecting altogether. We are social creatures by nature, connected with others from birth. From childhood, the need for acceptance, approval, affirmation, attention, and positive regard from our parents and others are some of our most fundamental psychological needs. Not having these needs met in one's life results in the unpleasant experience of rejection, and ultimately the inordinate fear of and sensitivity to situations that present this risk.

When we prospect, we take a huge emotional risk. We don't know how the prospect will respond. Will they yell at me? Will they hang up on me? We refuse to find out. The risk of embarrassment and rejection is too great. Many would rather risk their life than make a prospecting phone call.

I can't recall where I first heard it, but there is a story about a military recruiter who first built his career in the Marines and made a name for himself on the battlefield. Facing death every day was normal for him, and something he did without fear or hesitation. After returning from war, he took a position as a military recruiter. On his first day out of training, his mission was to contact 25 potential recruits. He was given a list of recent high school graduates who showed interest in the military, and he was asked to call them. The Marine was paralyzed by fear. He could not bring himself to make one prospecting phone call because his fear of rejection was too much for him to handle. This Marine, who stood six-feet-four-inches and weighed in at 230 pounds, and who had previously risked his life daily, was too scared to make prospecting calls to 18-year-old high school students and was reassigned. The fear of rejection is real! This book will show you how to overcome that fear.

2. Addiction to Instant Gratification

The second reason real estate agents don't prospect is thanks in part to social media, Amazon, and Netflix. We have become addicted to the instant gratification these platforms provide. Why? Dopamine, and a lot of it! Dopamine is a neurotransmitter—a chemical in the brain—that is released to make us feel pleasure and to keep us motivated. Dopamine causes you to want, desire, seek out, and satisfy your cravings. Activities that release large amounts of dopamine become the things we're most addicted to. Scrolling on social media, binge-watching television shows, eating sugar, dousing your food with sauces, sex, watching porn, and doing drugs, are just a few of these addictions.

The more we participate in activities that release large quantities of dopamine, the higher our dopamine tolerance becomes, increasing the amount required to feel pleasure. This is why people who consume alcohol on a regular basis require large amounts of alcohol to get drunk, whereas someone who rarely drinks will get drunk after one drink. This is how the scientists hired by social media companies have designed their platforms. Everything on social media is built to get you "hooked." Every time you get that notification, you look to see what it is. This activity gives you an instant hit of dopamine. The same thing happens when someone "likes" or comments on your social media posts.

The problem with increased dopamine tolerance is that activities that don't release as much dopamine don't interest you any longer, seem boring, and become much more difficult to do. This is why people would rather scroll on social media than go to the gym. It's not just you—it's all humans. Activities that offer instant results release a higher level of dopamine, whereas activities that don't offer results right away offer very little.

That's right, the speed with which you derive pleasure from an activity is purely a function of dopamine, and the same goes for the opposite. Activities that offer very little instant gratification result in very little dopamine, making these activities less desirable.

So when we look at the activity of prospecting, it's boring, mundane, filled with pain-wrenching rejection, and offers no immediate payoff. This is why so many real estate agents struggle to consistently prospect. But the long-term payoff from prospecting will lift your business, increase your income, and ultimately improve your life. Like most things in life, things that bring pleasure to you now are likely to cause pain later, and things that cause pain now will bring you pleasure in the future. Take exercise for example. No one likes waking up early and going to the gym; it's early, it's painful, and there's no immediate payoff. Only for those who commit to a life of health and fitness long-term will there be massive payoffs in the future. The same is true for those who choose short-term pleasure by sleeping in and eating doughnuts, because they will ultimately pay the price in the long term.

Later in the book, I'll teach you how to push through the pain and help you create a new habit of daily prospecting, but for now, my recommendation is to go on a dopamine detox. Start to limit activities that offer instant gratification so that your dopamine tolerance is reduced. This way, when you do things that seem hard to you right now, like prospecting, they will offer more enjoyment.

3. Becoming Easily Distracted

The opposite of distraction is focus. Being a great prospector requires insane amounts of focus and discipline. Now that you have a new awareness around why it's so hard to prospect consistently, your mind will be looking for ways to distract you while you're prospecting. Prospecting is an activity that causes most people pain and anxiety, and so they unconsciously look for distractions, depending on their level of dopamine addiction.

Rarely do agents admit it, but the truth is that most of us are actually seeking out distraction. Just hear me out. Distractions during prospecting let us off the hook and give us a reason to stop prospecting. We then turn around and want to make excuses why we can't hit our daily prospecting goals because of all the distractions, when in fact, we are the distraction.

Let me give you an example that I'm willing to bet you experience every day. As you're prospecting, your phone rings, (which it shouldn't because your phone should be on "Do Not Disturb" during your prospecting time block). But nonetheless, it's a client you're currently working with. Most untrained agents pick up the phone immediately and they justify this behavior as giving great client service and then classify this as a "distraction." In reality, this is exactly what the agent was hoping for. Instead of letting the call go to voicemail, like every other professional would do, the agent unconsciously rationalizes this decision as a legitimate excuse to stop prospecting. It's interesting when you stop to think about this. Imagine you're undergoing brain surgery. What if, all of a sudden the phone rings in the operating room and the doctor abruptly stops what he is doing and picks up the call because it could be a patient that has a question? Now, let's be real. I think you would agree that is absurd and would never happen in real life. But this is the type of behavior that happens all the time in the real estate industry.

"Current clients are calling me, vendors need me, my deal is blowing up, people are constantly knocking on my door," are all reasons I hear almost every day from agents as to why they can't prospect. It's not that these reasons are not important, but I want you to think about this from a different angle. When a current client sends you a text message during the time you've blocked out for prospecting and you answer the text, what was the real distraction? Be honest! First, it was your cell phone that was present in your prospecting station (which it should not be—more on that later), and second, it was you who responded to the text. Both of these were a byproduct of your decisions. I would make the argument that you are your biggest distraction. Every time the phone rings or someone knocks on the door, you have a choice how you'll respond. Keep in mind, your subconscious wants you to answer the phone call, answer the text, respond to the person at your door—anything to get a dopamine hit.

Be aware of this and build your "NO" power. This means you'll want to start saying "NO" to things that you're used to saying "YES" to now. The quick run to Starbucks with a colleague, the quick text response, the quick "Got a second?" conversation that always takes more than a minute. Start saying NO.

You also want to build a prospecting station that blocks external distractions. No media at all! And, if you can, make your prospecting calls in an environment that promotes productivity. DO NOT make prospecting calls around people who don't prospect. It's too tempting to stop prospecting to see what they're doing and it's too easy for you to fall victim to being judged by non-prospectors. If you have to prospect from your office, and don't have a private office, get a sign that says, "Do Not Disturb, Prospecting In Session." If you have to use your cell phone to make your calls, put it on "do not disturb" so phone calls and text messages won't tempt you.

4. Creative Avoidance

Many real estate agents convince themselves that there are tasks in their business that take priority over prospecting. Let me be clear and blunt: There's nothing more important in your business than prospecting—nothing.

Many real estate agents are plagued with "What-if? Syndrome." They often say things like, "I need to work on my website because what if a prospect looks me up online?" Or, "I need to work on my branding because what if I actually set an appointment with a prospect? I need to make a great impression with my logo, presentation folders, and business cards." And there are a million other things that real estate agents deem necessary before they can start prospecting. Even if an agent procrastinates for months, building their perfect website, designing the sexiest business cards, and finally gets to the point where they're about to make their calls, they spend hours researching the lead before they ever make the call. They do anything to avoid doing the actual work. This is called creative avoidance.

It's not that having a nice website or having your branding look good isn't important—it's just that these should not take priority over prospecting. These creative tasks should help support your prospecting but worked on only after your prospecting commitments have been met. Being a successful real estate agent has much more to do with your skills than what your website looks like or how fancy your logo is.

Don't believe me? I'll prove it. My best year as a real estate salesperson was in 2014 when I sold over 100 homes and earned over $600,000 in commission. The best part? I did this with NO website, NO social media pages and NO branding whatsoever. I did it through hard work, consistent prospecting, and crafting my skills as a salesperson. Never once did I have a prospect tell me the reason they are not doing business with me was because I didn't have a sexy website. Yet real estate agents are obsessed with doing everything in their business BUT prospecting.

Let's get the record straight: Your job as a real estate agent is to prospect for new business. If you want to build websites or design logos, change your career, because believe me when I tell you, if you don't prospect and spend your time avoiding it, you won't have a choice.

IF YOU DON'T PROSPECT, YOU'RE SELFISH

Most real estate agents will tell you the same thing when it comes to servicing their clients: When they have a client, they do everything they can to give that client a great experience. Their motivation to do so makes sense: To keep the client long-term and to get the client to give them referrals. But this is the easy part. The problem for most real estate agents isn't client service, it's the fact that they don't have enough clients to serve in the first place.

If you're like most, you would probably make the case that if a prospect decides to do business with you, they will have a great experience. Therefore, if you don't prospect, you're selfish! If you allow fear to hold you back from picking up the phone to call prospects who you already know need your help, you're selfish, or worse yet, full of shit. Maybe you don't give great service to your clients or get your clients the results you promise. For most though, I don't think this is the case. It's more likely that you don't prospect because of your fear.

Allow this new perspective to help you build a new habit of daily prospecting. Tell yourself, "There are people out there who need my help and if I don't call them, a competitor (who's not as good as me) will."

THE LEARNING IS IN THE DOING

"Just Do It," the famous Nike slogan, might be the best advice ever given. For centuries, society has suggested that we learn best by obtaining new information. The most successful people on the planet would disagree and so would I.

"Knowledge is power" is a lie that's been told for years. Information has no value without implementation. Have you ever thought about this? Doctors spend an average of 14 years learning about the human body before they ever become a fully licensed practitioner. Doctors arguably know more about health and the human body than anyone else on earth. But according to a physicians' health study, research shows that nearly 40% of the world's physicians are overweight and unhealthy. Doesn't this strike you to be a bit odd? This is concrete evidence that just because a person knows what to do does not mean they will do it.

The learning is in the doing. Although this book will teach you prospecting tactics and strategies that will make selling easy and fun, it will mean nothing if you don't actually do it. Applying the lessons in this book will bring you, your business, and your life much more value than simply just reading the words themselves.

WHY OUTBOUND PHONE PROSPECTING IS STILL KING

There are many ways to prospect and generate leads. You can door knock, join networking groups, engage on social media, buy leads, and send direct mail, just to name a few. They all work if you do the work. But nothing compares to direct, outbound phone calls. Here's why.

1. **Your energy and effort will be in the right place**

With direct outbound phone prospecting, you get to decide who you call; therefore, you will be calling prospects who you know with 100% certainty have a need to buy or sell a home. With other methods like networking, door knocking or direct mail, it's more of a shotgun approach. You're communicating with the masses, hoping to find someone interested in selling, and hope is not a strategy.

2. **It's the most effective and efficient use of your time**

For every hour you spend making outbound prospecting phone calls to a targeted list, you can literally speak to eight to 10 of the exact prospects you're looking for. On average, depending on your sales skills, you can generate one or two highly qualified leads as a result of these conversations and only one hour of your time. There's nothing—and let me repeat nothing—that can even come close to competing with these types of results.

There's no magic bullet or marketing gimmick that can generate eight to 10 actual conversations with motivated homeowners in the next 60 minutes. Trust me—if there was, you'd know about it and so would everyone else.

So why doesn't everyone make outbound prospecting calls? Here's the truth: it's hard, grueling, boring work that most are not willing to endure. Those who do, however, will live a life that most can only dream of. Like the great Jim Rohn said, "Don't wish it were easier, wish you were better." This makes sense: If it were easy, you'd have a lot more agents to compete with. Even though it may not feel like it at times, only a very small portion of the real estate agents actually prospect daily. Here's some proof. Go ask the agents in your brokerage or on your company Facebook page how many agents call FSBOs, expired listings, or FRBOs every day? You'll be pleasantly surprised to find out that you may be the only one in your company willing to do the hard work. Here's the good news: If you actually do the work that daily prospecting requires, you'll be alone at the top of all the leaderboards at your company and in your market.

THE FOUR STAGES OF PROSPECTING MASTERY

There are four stages of learning that everyone goes through when learning something new and there are no exceptions when it comes to mastering the art and science of prospecting. You, like everyone who has come before you, must go through these four stages to reach mastery. There are no shortcuts or ways to avoid them. You must pay the price at each stage to reach the top.

Stage 1—Unconscious Incompetence

In stage one, you're filled with excitement to start something new like starting a new job or new relationship. It's the excitement that sparks action. This will most likely happen as a result of this book. After going through this book, you'll likely have the motivation to get on the phone and start building the life of your dreams. You don't know what you don't know and you're just excited to get started!

Stage 2—Conscious Incompetence

This is the stage where most quit. Once the pain or reality sets in that this is hard work and results are not immediate, you'll quickly find yourself looking for the path of least resistance. You'll find yourself looking for other things to do so that prospecting can be avoided. You'll be frustrated that you're not getting the results you desire.

It is critical and your career depends on you pushing through this phase of deception. It's normal to suck in the beginning as you're growing your skills. It's like anything in life that you start with little or no experience. Prospecting and selling is no different. Embrace the suck and love the pain because the life you desire is waiting for you on the other side.

Stage 3—Conscious Competence

If you're one of the few who successfully pushes through the dreadful stage 2, you'll find yourself starting to have success. It's still hard, but you're now starting to get better, generating some leads and even setting some face-to-face appointments. Although the phone still may weigh 1,000 pounds in this phase, as soon as you get past your first call, you'll find yourself starting to get results. These results will bring the excitement back and give you the motivation to keep going!

Stage 4—Unconscious Competence

It's in this stage where you've reached mastery. You can pick up the phone, generate leads and set appointments with ease and without very much effort. It's like driving a car or riding a bike for most adults. For example, your competence with riding a bike is so high, it's likely that you could stop what you're doing right now, go anywhere in the world and jump on a bike and start riding without much effort. This level of mastery only comes through repetition. Although it may take you years to get here, if you don't give up, you will get here. And when you do, you will have forgotten how hard it was to start. At this point it's likely that your income and life are a reflection of all your hard work.

3
The Prospecting Millionaire Mindset

THE 80/15/5 PRINCIPLE

In almost 20 years of leading salespeople, building multiple businesses, and interviewing some of the leading minds in the sales industry, I've learned that succeeding in sales comes down to three core things: mindset, action, and skills—in that order.

All three are critical to whether or not one will succeed or fail as a salesperson. Mindset, however, makes up 80% of your success, while actions make up 15%, and skills, although important, make up only 5%. Here's why.

Your mindset controls how you feel, which affects your attitude. Your attitude then impacts the choices you make, which ultimately leads to the amount of action you take daily. How many times have you said to yourself, "I just don't feel like it"? This is a death sentence to your productivity. So if you're going to succeed, it's critical that you learn how to strengthen your mindset.

In this chapter we will review 10 mindsets that real estate agents who earn more than $1 million a year in net income all share. These are the mindsets that, if mastered, have the power to help you become a world class salesperson and a top-producing real estate agent.

MINDSET 1
HAVE THE COURAGE TO ASK FOR WHAT YOU WANT

You'll never reach your potential in sales if you don't get over the fact that you must ask prospects for what you want. The reason most real estate agents don't ask prospects for what they want (the appointment, a referral, to sign the contract), is because they don't want to come across as a pushy salesperson, which I completely understand. This book will teach you exactly how to ask for what you want in a way that is collaborative with the prospect and does not come across "salesy." But make no mistake, you must ask.

Believe it or not, and contrary to popular belief, prospects will actually give you more respect when you're transparent, direct, and honest about what you want. It's when the prospect feels like you're beating around the bush that they start to push back, give you more resistance, and lose respect.

Starting today, have the courage to ask for what you want and ask for it with confidence, even if at first it makes you feel uncomfortable. This mindset and habit will be something you will benefit from for the rest of your career and the rest of your life.

MINDSET 2
DETACH FROM THE OUTCOME 100%

Obviously we all want to achieve the goals we've set, but unless we're focused on the actions, behaviors, and skills necessary, our goals will always elude us. Too many untrained real estate agents come off as needy or desperate, which prospects can smell a mile away. This is called "commission breath." When you're desperate to make a sale, you become "salesy," which repels the prospect, and they end up doing the exact opposite of what you want.

To convert more prospects into clients you must detach from the outcome 100%. The prospect should never know your cards. When communicating, the prospect should almost feel as though the "sale" is the least of your concerns.

Stay calm, keep your emotions under control, and always seek to understand. You know when you're detached from the outcome when you have standards in your business and you actually follow them by saying "No" to prospects when the old you said "Yes" every time ("Yes" to discounted commission, bad terms, and unreasonable requests). Prospects of the past owned the old you, and you know it. Detaching from the outcome is when you can look the prospect in the eye and tell them the absolute truth about helping them achieve their desired outcome without worrying about losing the deal. The truth is, this is what your prospects want. And once you have built the confidence and courage to execute, there will be no limits to how successful you can become. Being 100% detached from the outcome truly means you're not concerned with whether or not you close the deal, and the prospect knows it.

MINDSET 3
THE PROSPECTING LAW OF THE HARVEST

There's no denying that we all want results quickly, but only a few understand how results actually manifest. Obtaining results with prospecting, as well as with sales in general, is a lot like working out. Gaining the results you want will take much more time than you think, be much more difficult than you had initially thought, and only a small percentage will remain consistent enough for long enough to reap the rewards.

One of my favorite books of all time, a book that changed the way I look at everything in life, is called *The Compound Effect* by Darren Hardy. He tells a great story of the compounding penny. If you've never heard this powerful story, I'll sum it up for you. If you were given a choice between getting $3 million today or getting one penny that doubled every day for 31 days, which would you pick? Whether you've heard this story before or not, you can probably guess most people would choose the $3 million due to their dopamine addiction. That would be a bad choice, and here's why.

On day one, if you chose to receive the $3 million, it might seem like a great choice at first. Even after 20 days, your choice seems as though it's paid off, for if you had chosen the penny, you'd only have $5,243. Then, the magic of the compound effect and law of the harvest kick in. On day 29, if you had chosen the penny it would compound to $2.7 million, then double on day 30 to $5.4 million, and then double again on day 31 resulting in a grand total of a whopping $10,737,418.24. The point is this: Small positive choices made daily, that seem almost insignificant in the moment, are the very choices that create success long term.

This is the secret to prospecting and winning in business. Agents who struggle are inconsistent in everything they do, but after reading this book, you will have the mindset and skills to prospect daily, regardless of the outcome. Over time you'll have a bigger pipeline of prospects and clients than anyone in your company and be on your way to reaching your fullest potential.

MINDSET 4
PAY THE PRICE EVERY DAY, NO MATTER WHAT

"I just don't feel like prospecting today" must be something you never tell yourself again. Prospecting is paying the price today for what you want in the future. Results in sales are not instant and often don't show up until months after we've done the work. Every day you decide not to prospect will result in delaying your income for months. Remember the compound effect and law of the harvest? Well, they can work against you too. Forget delaying your income—if you go too many days without prospecting, you'll find yourself being forced to find a new career.

MINDSET 5
AVOID CREATIVE AVOIDANCE

Salespeople are great at selling themselves on doing anything besides their actual job, which is to prospect. Marketing, branding, and technology companies know this and have profited massively from distracting real estate agents. We create a story in our mind that there are tasks in our business that take priority over prospecting that we must get done now. As mentioned earlier, nothing in your business is more important than prospecting—nothing.

Real estate agents convince themselves that their website must be perfect before they can make their first call. They also tell themselves that their current logo will somehow hold them back from succeeding; and therefore, they justify spending weeks designing a new logo and pretend as though they are being productive. This is creative avoidance. Prospecting is your number 1 priority and everything else should be secondary. Creative avoidance is a form of analysis paralysis, which has been said to be procrastination in disguise.

Once you've adopted this mindset and start prospecting daily while putting your to-do list on the sideline for now, you'll be amazed to find out those projects you thought were mission-critical end up meaning nothing most of the time. You'll find yourself setting more appointments, closing more deals, and quickly forgetting about the sexy presentation folders with the new logo you've been designing for weeks.

Trust me, over time, you'll learn your skills will be the reason why prospects do business with you and not because of the texture on your business card.

MINDSET 6
HAVE AN UNWAVERING COMMITMENT

Real estate agents are known for having shiny object syndrome, bouncing from one tactic or strategy to another and never sticking to anything long term. They spend countless hours listening to podcasts and watching YouTube videos of people promising they can succeed without prospecting. So they try it, and I mean everything. The key word here being "try." Trying means that you've given up before you've even started.

Let's be honest: Do Facebook ads work? Sure. Does direct mail still work? Absolutely. Can you get business from Google pay-per-click campaigns? For sure. The issue is that most real estate agents don't have enough money to spend on these campaigns for a long enough time for them to actually turn a profit.

When you learn how to effectively prospect, you'll never have to worry where your next deal is coming from, and you'll never have to spend thousands on expensive marketing campaigns again. Will it be hard? Yes. Will it take time? Absolutely. Will you want to quit? Of course. But for those who commit to mastering the Reverse Selling Method and prospect every day will always find themselves on top of the leaderboard.

Just look around: The top real estate agents at every company are the agents who have the best work ethic and the biggest pipelines of new prospects and referrals. Why? It's simple. They got there through years of consistent daily prospecting. If this is what you desire, you must have an unwavering commitment to daily prospecting. Keep your head down and do the work. There are no magic pills, no magic formulas, and no secrets. The only secret is that top agents prospect daily, no matter what, no matter how they feel, while most do not.

MINDSET 7
HAVE BLIND FAITH THAT WHAT YOU'RE DOING WILL WORK

If you're new to prospecting, it's normal for you to have doubts and get frustrated. At times, you'll probably even think that direct prospecting doesn't work. Let me assure you, there's nothing in sales that works better than direct outbound phone prospecting. I've made millions of dollars in commissions, most of which was a direct result from making outbound prospecting phone calls. If that's not enough, I've coached, trained, and interviewed hundreds of real estate agents earning more than $250,000 a year in net income and some even earning over $1 million a year, and one thing is true: They are fanatical about prospecting. On the other hand, there are thousands of real estate agents who are obsessed with chasing shiny objects and marketing gimmicks, who are broke, stressed out, and on the verge of changing careers. The only thing standing in your way to achieving your greatest potential in real estate is your willingness to commit to daily prospecting and developing your sales skills.

MINDSET 8
SUCCESSFUL PEOPLE ARE NO DIFFERENT THAN YOU

When I first started my career, I used to think that the super-achievers knew something I didn't know, or were doing something I didn't know how to do. I've since learned through my own successes and failures the only difference between top agents and everyone else is not that they know something you don't, it's that they execute on these simple fundamentals every day while you do not. There's no better example of this than Vince Lombardi, the Hall of Fame NFL coach of the Green Bay Packers. His teams were so good at executing on the fundamentals that their competition knew exactly what they were going to do and still could not stop them. This was a breakthrough for me and I hope it will have the same impact for you. It's true! The super-achievers in life, whether in sales, business, sports, dancing, or singing, all hate doing the hard work, but they do it anyway. They push past the pain, eliminate excuses, and do the work, regardless of how they feel.

MINDSET 9
ACCEPT THE FACT THAT YOU, AND YOU ALONE, ARE 100% RESPONSIBLE FOR YOUR RESULTS

If you're not succeeding or achieving at the level you desire, I can promise you it's not because the leads are bad, or because you're at the wrong company or because of who is elected president. It's none of these, nor is it any other excuse you tell yourself. It's actually pretty simple. If you're not achieving your income goals as a real estate agent, it's because you don't have enough quality prospects in your pipeline due to your lack of prospecting. Yup, that's it. Victims make excuses and always have a reason why not, while winners own their results because it gives them the power. Victims are powerless and will always be subject to their circumstances while going through life, never knowing they held the power to change their life the whole time.

You and you alone are responsible for the actions you take and the results you achieve. Once you've accepted this fact, you'll have the power to achieve any life you desire.

MINDSET 10
BE-TO-HAVE VS. HAVE-TO-BE

Most of us live with a "Have-to-Be" mindset. I have to be with the right company before I can succeed. I have to be at the right college to get a good job. I have to be with the right crowd to be accepted. I have to be wealthy to attract the right spouse—and the list goes on forever. Here's the truth: Most people will never have what they desire with this mindset. To achieve what we desire, we must adopt a new mindset of "Be-to-Have." This is a mindset of becoming the type of person you want to be today to have what you want in the future.

As an example, what kind of person do you think earns $1 million a year? I think we would agree it's someone who is disciplined, focused, and does the hard work, day in and day out. It only makes sense that if we chose to become this person of discipline and focus, it will only be a matter of time before we achieve these same results. Money and numbers follow, they don't lead. Think about it. Maybe this is the reason most of us will never achieve the things we've sought out to achieve. Living a "Have-to-Be" lifestyle is another form of victim mentality. It suggests you're not in control of your destiny, and that only when something happens to you can you achieve your desired outcomes in life.

4
The 23 Rules of Reverse Selling

To start learning the Reverse Selling Method you must first understand the 23 fundamental principles and rules of Reverse Selling. These principles act as the foundation of Reverse Selling and will guide you to becoming a world-class real estate agent, making prospecting something that is fun and easy. Once mastered, the days of being filled with fear will be behind you and calling prospects will be something you look forward to doing.

RULE #1
NOTHING IS AS IT SEEMS

Prospects lie, mislead, and tell you anything to get you off the phone. Why? You're a salesperson and people don't trust you! So when a prospect gives you an objection or shows resistance, stop taking it personally, stop getting defensive, and stop trying to sell them by trying to convince them they are wrong! You will lose every time.

For example, when I was growing my career in the real estate sales business and would call For Sale by Owners (FSBOs) to see if they might need help selling their home, they would give the same objection almost every time: "I'm not interested in working with a real estate agent."

Now, for years I did the same thing most untrained agents are doing now, which is to try to overcome their objections by convincing them that working with a Realtor was better than selling their house by owner. How do you think that worked out? That's right, it didn't. Most of the time, the prospect who was selling their home by owner would hang up on me. But it got even worse. Not even 30 days would go by and I would see the same prospect had their home listed with a competing agent!

I realized what prospects told me over the phone was rarely what they meant. In fact, most of the time, it was the exact opposite. It was just their reflex resistance talking. It's the same thing when we all say, "Just looking," after the greeter at the department store asks, "Can I help you find something?" Give me a break. As if we were so bored that we went out of our way and drove to a specific store just to look? I don't think so. We just say this as a reflex, without even thinking about it.

This rule teaches us not to take a prospect's resistance literally, but rather to stay agreeable and ask other hypothetical questions to dig for their true motivation (you'll learn how to do this later in the book).

RULE #2
A FACE-TO-FACE MEETING CHANGES EVERYTHING

The purpose of a prospecting phone call is to set a face-to-face appointment, period. Sales "gurus" have taught us for years that we should "qualify, qualify, qualify" before we set an appointment.

This is some of the worst advice ever given to real estate agents, and here's why. Think about this from the prospect's point of view: When a complete stranger calls them to sell them something, what incentive do they have to give them any information over the phone? Oh that's right—none! Prospects will never give you the whole story over the phone, but a face-to-face meeting changes everything.

Millions of dollars in commissions are lost every year because real estate agents are taking what prospects say over the phone literally rather than focusing on getting face to face. Prospects are much more likely to open up to you at a face-to-face meeting than over the phone. Stop overqualifying on the prospecting call, looking for reasons not to set an appointment, and start looking for reasons to get a face-to-face meeting scheduled! I promise when you change this strategy in your business, your listings will increase dramatically.

RULE #3
SEEK OUT, EMBRACE, AND VALUE REJECTION

"I've missed more than 9,000 shots in my career, I've lost almost 300 games, 26 times I've been trusted to take the game winning shot and missed. I've failed over, and over, and over again in my life. And that is why I succeed."
Michael Jordan

You see, the key to becoming a great prospector and top real estate agent is to get more rejection than your competition is willing to endure. Why? When you have more experience on the battlefield than anyone else, your skills are forced to improve. This is what many people don't understand. The learning is in the doing, and not in some textbook. It's not that role play and practice are not important in sales, but nothing can give you the experience you need to develop your skills like a real prospecting call. The more calls you make the more rejection you'll get, and as a result, your skills will sharpen and your income will skyrocket. It's that simple.

RULE #4
YOU ARE WHO YOU HANG OUT WITH MOST OF THE TIME

It's true that birds of a feather flock together. This is particularly true with real estate agents. As I discussed in Chapter 3, mindset is everything. If you hang out with negative people, non-prospectors, and low producers, you can't help but become like them. I'll prove it to you. Here's a little experiment for you to try. Go to lunch with two of your friends who are health and fitness fanatics. I guarantee you that after they order their grilled chicken salads with water, you don't order your usual cheeseburger with fries and a beer. We're social creatures and have a need to be accepted by the herd. This is why it's so powerful to surround yourself with people who are achieving at the level at which you also wish to achieve. It's not magic, it's science. To fit in, you also need to succeed at their level to be accepted—and succeed you will!

RULE #5
YOUR RESULTS ARE A DIRECT REFLECTION OF YOUR DAILY SCHEDULE

Superman's weakness is kryptonite. The real estate agent's kryptonite, without any debate, is and will always be time management. Most real estate agents are paid based on performance and therefore have schedules that allow for flexibility, unlike people who are paid based on their time. This causes a massive problem for agents who are unconsciously and unintentionally going about their day-to-day. On the contrary, real estate agents who have the most disciplined daily schedules will always outproduce those agents who don't follow a schedule. When humans are given a choice between doing hard things and doing easy things, nine times out of 10, we choose the path of least resistance.

In my online coaching business ReverseSelling.com, we teach our coaching clients that 70% of their day should be spent in revenue-generating activities; that means prospecting and going on appointments. The tighter your schedule, the more money you will earn.

RULE #6
FEEDBACK IS A GIFT

Sometimes we are unaware of the areas in our business or our life that are most in need of improvement, which an outsider's perspective can often reveal to us. If you're lucky enough to have a good mentor or coach who gives you feedback, it can be difficult to accept this at first. Accepting feedback is as much of a skill as is delivering it. You may not always like the feedback. You may not agree with it. But make no mistake, feedback is a gift. Someone saw something that might make you better and had the courage to tell you about it. There's great value in this and it would be wise for you to listen.

RULE #7
YOU SELL THE WAY YOU BUY

Real estate agents have an unconscious tendency to sell the way they buy. If you're the type of person who's always looking for a deal, it's more likely you'll agree when your prospects ask you to discount your commission. Or you may find yourself often "haggling" over price with your prospects. If you're the type of person who takes a long time to make decisions, it's likely that you will get many prospects who give you the "I want to think it over" objection. Look at yourself as a consumer and analyze your behavior. If you don't like how prospects respond to you, it's probably because you sell the way you buy.

Here's an example. Let's say you're the type of person who has a tough time making decisions, and when prospects tell you they need time to "think it over," rather than isolate the objection (which you'll learn about later in the book), you take this literally and let prospects off the hook. Change your buying habits and you can also change the way in which you sell, which will ultimately impact how your prospects respond.

RULE #8
MASTER SELF-DISCIPLINE, FOCUS, AND MENTAL TOUGHNESS

Winning in real estate is much like winning in the game of life in that it takes self-discipline, focus, and mental toughness. Though many people over-complicate what it takes to succeed, the truth is, succeeding in real estate is very basic, very simple, and comes down to executing on a few fundamentals. It's not fancy scripts or sexy marketing campaigns that will get you to the top: It's your ability to execute on the boring, mundane, daily prospecting that is required, staying focused in a world of distractions, and having the perseverance to never give up or give in to the temptations so many others fall victim to.

RULE #9
NEVER TAKE THE BAIT

Real estate agents have been misguided and given horrible advice for years. They've been taught when a prospect gives an objection or resistance on a prospecting call, they should try to "overcome" that objection by convincing the prospect that what they said is not valid and that they are in fact wrong.

The issue with attempting to overcome objections on prospecting calls is that, if done incorrectly, which is more often the case than not, the agent loses the opportunity before they even get started. We call this taking the bait. The next time a prospect responds with reflex resistance, or gives you an objection, don't take the bait and jump all over it like every other untrained salesperson. Instead, use a pattern interrupt and agree. Yes, that's not a typo, I said "agree" with the prospect! I know, you're probably saying to yourself, "What!? That goes against everything I know about sales!" That's the point. Remember, your goal while prospecting is to identify potential prospects, and when you do, to move that prospect forward in your sales process. That's it. Ideally, this should be done with a face-to-face meeting scheduled, or at least with a follow-up phone call at an agreed upon time in the future. Trying to talk them out of their objections over the phone is a good way not to do that.

A pattern interrupt, by the way, is a communication device meant to do just that—interrupt typical behavior patterns that the prospect is used to engaging in without thinking about it. When your prospect gives you an objection, they fully expect you to come back and try to sell them, which is what you've been taught to do and were planning on doing, right? Well, when you use a pattern interrupt and agree with the prospect's objection or resistance, they are stunned! They don't know how to respond and their defense mechanisms are torn down in a matter of seconds, and they can't understand why. This allows you to accomplish your goal in the prospecting call, which is to move the prospect forward in your sales process. Get it?

Here's an example. Let's pretend you call a FSBO and they say, "Thanks for calling but we're not interested in working with an agent at this time." Instead of taking the bait, like you've been doing your whole career, and pitching the prospect on why it's better to sell with an agent (while the prospect holds the phone away from their ear), use a pattern interrupt and say, "That makes sense, there's no reason why you shouldn't be able to sell your house on your own." This is when the magic happens. The prospect is caught totally off guard, like a deer in headlights, which allows you to remove the prospects' initial reflex resistance and gives you an opportunity to move the prospect forward.

For the first time in your real estate career (probably) you can see how you can get prospects to listen to and respect you on the phone without having to fight the uphill battle of trying to overcome all of their objections.

RULE #10
NEVER ARGUE ON A PROSPECT CALL

Are prospects rude from time to time? Yes. Are prospects great at listening? No! Will you get frustrated on prospecting calls? Yes, all the time. You must, however, control your emotions and never, ever, argue on a prospecting call! It serves absolutely no strategic purpose and virtually guarantees that you will lose a potential prospect. Now that you've learned to never take the bait by staying agreeable with the prospect and never arguing, you will find it easier to remain in control of your emotions and thus in control of the entire phone call (more on that later).

RULE #11
NEVER TAKE REFLEX RESISTANCE LITERALLY

Remember, decades of pushy sales tactics have caused people to have a built-in, automatic, defense mechanism toward salespeople. Even as a real estate agent, you too have this unconscious defense system. I gave the example in Rule #1 about responding "Just looking" whenever a department store salesperson approaches to ask if you needed help. It's simply your defense system at work. Here, watch what happens next to prove this point. Just minutes later after saying, "No I'm just looking," you're standing at the cash register paying for the product you're buying. Or scenario two after responding to the salesperson with your reflex resistance, you go seek out that very salesperson to ask for help finding something in the store. Does anyone find this as fascinating as I do?

This proves that as salespeople, we cannot take the prospects' reflex resistance literally. We have to stay agreeable using pattern interrupts to allow us to move the conversation forward.

RULE #12
CONSISTENCY IS KING

Like anything in life, obtaining the results we want takes time. If you were to ask the world's elite athletes, singers, business leaders, and entrepreneurs for their best advice, there's little doubt that "consistency" would be among the most common answers given. The same is true for prospecting and building your real estate business. In Chapter 3 you learned about the Law of the Harvest and The Compound Effect. Well, the only way to positively benefit from the law of the harvest is to do the work every day without fail! There's no other way around this simple truth. If there was, I'd know about it and I would tell you. In fact, everything in sales comes down to your ability to be consistent in everything you do; role play and practice, prospect, and follow up with leads in your pipeline. It's no surprise that salespeople who are the most consistent in these activities are always the top producers. There's no reason why the same can't also be true for you.

RULE #13
DON'T BE THE LITTLE BOY ON PROM NIGHT

Once you understand the Reverse Selling Method strategies outlined in this book and you've also mastered how to ask Socratic-style questions, you'll have prospects eating out of your hands and explaining to you their problems and issues in vivid detail—problems your product or service could help solve for them. It's critical, however, that you learn not to pounce on this opportunity right away and start "selling." You'll lose the prospect's trust and everything you've achieved up to this point.

Here's an example of what most untrained agents do: Let's pretend you're a real estate agent and you're meeting with a potential client looking to list their home for sale. Through asking a series of strategic questions, you get the prospect to open up and tell you all the reasons they were not happy with their prior agent. One of the things they tell you is that their last agent was bad at keeping them updated on the process. An untrained salesperson jumps all over this and starts spewing out how "great they are at communication" and how they will "keep them updated the entire way." This very non-strategic sales tactic is what we call a "setup" and shows the agent has short-term thinking, is needy for a sale, and comes across as very desperate. When we act this way, the prospect quickly retracts, holds their cards closer, and loses trust. This behavior is like the little boy on prom night who has no self-control. Don't do it.

RULE #14
DON'T FALL FOR THE MIRAGE OF HOPE

Over the years, prospects have learned some great counter-tactics that allow them to get rid of salespeople. In some cases, the prospect has stronger skills than the salesperson! Here's an example prospects use all the time and one that works with most untrained salespeople. At the end of a sales meeting, the prospect says, "Bob, everything you said today makes sense and I think working together will be great. There are a few things I have to take care of before we move forward and I'll let you know the second I'm ready, fair enough?"

WHAT!? The prospect even used the F word! This works like a charm! The salesperson gets excited and falls for the mirage. The mirage the salesperson actually believes is that the prospect is interested and leaves in a hurry to respect the prospect and not do anything that might hurt their chances of winning the deal. HUGE MISTAKE!

You have not clarified next steps with the prospect so you go on "the chase." This is where you end up calling the prospect for months, chasing them down without ever hearing back. I know, it's painful. This is your fault. When a prospect responds this way, stay calm and ask the prospect a few more questions about how we should move forward.

We call this The Reverse Close, which you'll learn about in a later chapter. We need to get the prospect to tell us how we should proceed and what we should do next. Here's a quick example:

If a prospect ends a meeting with excitement, don't be excited. This is a common sign that the prospect may not actually be interested. Instead, you want to utilize one of the Reverse Selling skills we call The Reverse Close, and ask the prospect a question that gives the prospect an "out" to test for true motivation. You'll respond with, "I'm glad you're excited to do business but what about your agent? Will it be hard for you to switch to a new agent since you've been with them for so long?"

One of two things will happen. Either the prospect will defend their position and motivation for moving forward with you, which is a good sign, or they will tend to agree with the "out" you've given them. When this happens you know you have more work to do.

RULE #15
IF YOU FEEL SOMETHING, SAY SOMETHING

We've all been in situations where we've felt something is bothering the person we're talking with. This is your intuition—trust it. This is a very powerful gift we all need to use as real estate agents, and it's one of the best ways to connect with a prospect. You see, most untrained agents act like glorified customer service reps or a waiter or waitress. There's nothing wrong with that, but it's hard to have a real connection with someone when you know the other person will basically agree with whatever you say. As humans, almost all of us have the gift of intuition and can truly feel the way other people are feeling—if we pay attention.

The next time you're talking with a prospect and you feel as though they are having some internal resistance, ask them if everything's OK. When they say

"Yes, why?" respond with, "Well, I get the feeling what we're discussing might not make sense for you right now. Am I right?" In the book *Never Split The Difference*, author Chris Voss calls this skill "labeling."

This will help you to humanize yourself with the prospect and pull out real potential concerns. This way, you and the prospect can have a deeper conversation about doing business together, and whether it makes sense to continue moving forward at this time.

RULE #16
TO INFLUENCE OTHERS, YOU MUST MASTER YOUR OWN EMOTIONS

In a typical conversation it's the one who is the most calm and usually the one asking the most questions who is in control. This is how you want to be at all times. The real masters of influence are those who can't be rattled, regardless of the situation. These are the people we call to negotiate with terrorists or close the billion-dollar deal. If you desire to be a person of influence and to be able to impact the decisions of others, you must first become a master at controlling your own emotions.

RULE #17
YOUR PAST CLIENTS ARE THE BEST SOURCE OF NEW BUSINESS

Many real estate agents are overly-transactional in the way they communicate with their clients. It's not until years later that they regret doing business this way. Believe me when I tell you, no one wants to wake up 20 or 30 years from now and have to still grind it out on the phone every day to find the next deal. Take care of your current clients in such a way that if your business was only able to grow by referrals from past clients, you'd still have a thriving business. Give your clients such an amazing experience when dealing with you that they can't help but rave about you to their friends, families, and coworkers. I also recommend you read *Raving Fans* by Ken Blanchard and Sheldon Bowles on this subject. There's no better way to get new business than through past client referrals. They've already done business with you and do all the selling for you! All you have to do is show up and not screw it up. Oh, and by the way, referrals are the most profitable lead source, by far.

RULE #18
NO PAIN, NO SALE

Real estate agents, as salespeople, have received a bad reputation with the general public from decades of convincing prospects to buy products and services they did not need. But this must change if real estate agents are going to earn the public's trust once again. After reading this book, you'll learn Reverse Selling is a process of understanding, not convincing. This means that we must practice one of Stephen Covey's core philosophies: "Seek first to understand, then to be understood." When—and only when—you've identified the prospect has pain or a need that your product or service can solve will you move forward. Otherwise, you're wasting your time and building enemies.

RULE #19
IF YOU'RE TELLING, YOU'RE NOT SELLING

The perfect talk/listen ratio is 70% listening and talking only 30% of the time. If you find yourself talking more than you are listening, it's likely you're falling into old selling habits and doing too much convincing. Selling should be a process of asking questions to identify the prospect's pain points and to determine whether your product or service can help. Once a need has been established, you should then move on to asking the prospect hypothetical questions about what things would be like if their need was solved. It should be the prospect who does the selling, not you.

RULE #20
HIGH, INTENSE ACCOUNTABILITY IS
THE KEY TO HIGH ACHIEVEMENT

Left on our own, humans will never perform as well as when we know people are watching. It's in our nature to take the path of least resistance. Our brains are hardwired to keep us safe and away from pain. So get someone to hold you accountable for doing the hard things you know are required to succeed in your business.

When it comes to physical fitness, it's no secret that reaching one's highest potential will require consistent training and a disciplined diet. Seeking the help of a trusted person to help hold them accountable to a daily workout routine is not uncommon for people who have this goal. Somehow, when people become real estate agents, they kind of forget the value of accountability. The secret to high performance is accountability. And all high-achieving real estate agents will tell you they're being held accountable to the highest level. If you were to interview the top 10 real estate agents in your market you'll find all 10 have a coach or someone holding them accountable to the goals they've set. On the opposite spectrum, if you were to interview the bottom 10 agents in the market, it's also true you'll find they have no one to hold them accountable. Let this be concrete evidence that accountability is the secret to high achievement. Because let's face it, left to your own devices, you're always going to take the path of least resistance.

Many people run away from accountability. They say things like, "I'm my own boss," "I don't need to be held accountable," or "I hold myself accountable." However, we have found that people who have this attitude are typically very insecure about holding to their commitments. They do not trust themselves to do the work consistently, and therefore do not run the risk of being exposed by having someone in their life hold them accountable. This is one of the secrets of super-achievers. People at the top of their game like Tiger Woods, Michael Jordan, and Venus and Serena Williams, all have private coaches to push them. The same goes for elite salespeople. Most top salespeople are being coached and held accountable to achieving the goals they've set. Who's holding you accountable?

RULE #21
THE PURPOSE OF A PROSPECTING CALL IS TO SET AN APPOINTMENT

Most sales cycles require more than one conversation. A big mistake I see untrained real estate agents make is that they try to force the sale too quickly on the first call. They over-qualify and look for a quick commitment from the prospect. This is another example of trying to take the path of least resistance. I get it—if you can call a prospect, qualify them, and get them to commit to buy your product or service on the very first call, great! Do it! This is something that tends to work great in theory, but in the real world of selling, you and I both know that converting a prospect into a client takes time.

But let's examine that theory a little closer to see if it actually works as well as some would suggest it does. Let's pretend you're single and your friend calls you and says, "Hey, I have a friend you have to meet! Here's her number. Call her." You call her for the first time and ask her on a date. She agrees to a first date and right before you hang up, you decide to take the advice that so many sales trainers give, and go for the close. You say, "Before I let you go, if the date goes well, and you like me and I like you, I'm planning to get on my knee and ask you to marry me right there on the spot. So are you willing to just go ahead and make that decision right now?" The woman would hang up the phone immediately, call the mutual friend, and give her an earful. She might even get a restraining order against you!

I know, this sounds ridiculous, but it's what so many salespeople do. Remember, the purpose of the prospecting call is to simply have a meeting to discuss the prospect's needs and determine if you can help. That's it!

RULE #22
PEOPLE DON'T CARE HOW MUCH YOU KNOW UNTIL THEY KNOW HOW MUCH YOU CARE

Sales is all about how you make people feel, not what you say. One of my mentors early in my career told me, "People don't care how much you know until they know how much you care." This could not be more true in sales.

Most real estate agents are guilty of feature-dumping and overwhelming their prospects with all of the details about their product or service, and thus all of the reasons why the prospect should do business with them. This is one of the biggest mistakes untrained salespeople make. Instead of asking questions to clarify misunderstanding, uncover areas of need, and dig for true motivation, they just start talking, falling victim to old sales tactics of trying to convince the person through features and benefits.

Your goal as a real estate agent is to actually care about your work and the results you get for your clients. If not, and it's all about the commission, this will be a very short-lived career for you. Succeeding in real estate is more about how we make people feel vs. just saying the words we think they want to hear. So many agents obsess over what script to use and wonder, "What do I say if they say this?" It's less about the words and more about our ability to connect with the consumer on such a level that they actually believe you care. Once that's established, you'll have a client for life and they will refer future clients to your business forever.

RULE #23
PROFESSIONALS TRACK THEIR NUMBERS

What gets measured gets improved. It's that simple. Want to lose weight? Write down and track everything you put in your mouth for a month and I guarantee you will make better choices. Want to cut back on spending? Write down every dollar you spend and again, I guarantee you'll spend less.

Could you imagine sports without stats? How many championships did Michael Jordan win? "We have no idea—we don't track that stuff." Give me a break! That's ridiculous. But the reality is, it's rare to find a salesperson who tracks their numbers. I know, it's crazy.

Think about this: If a salesperson does not track their numbers and is struggling to achieve their goals, how would they know which part of their business needs improving? Oh yeah, that's right—they wouldn't! That's the problem. Here's the value of tracking your numbers. Imagine a world where you know how many meetings it took you to get a new client, how many phone conversations it took to set a meeting, how many dials it took to have a conversation, and how many dials you could make per hour. You would establish a conversion ratio for each category and be able to know with absolute certainty how to achieve any goal you'd set. More on ratios later, but the point is this: Sales is a game and you need to know your numbers intimately. The better you know your numbers, the more motivated you'll be. Knowing where you stand provides you with the clarity you need to take action.

5

Reverse Selling Skills in Action

So far we've talked about the prospecting millionaire mindset, some general truths about prospecting, and the 23 rules of Reverse Selling. Now it's time to put the Reverse Selling Method into action. In this chapter you'll learn how to use different Reverse Selling skills in real selling situations. These skills will serve you well, turning prospecting into something you enjoy and making the entire selling process something you look forward to. And if that wasn't enough, your prospects will start to actually trust you as you earn their respect.

SKILL #1
REMOVING REFLEX RESISTANCE

As you make more and more prospecting phone calls, you'll naturally get used to reflex resistance. Reflex resistance, as I mentioned before, is when a prospect's natural defense system is triggered whenever they encounter a salesperson. It's something they don't even think about. To remove it, never forget Reverse Selling Rule #11—Never Take Reflex Resistance Literally, and second, follow this three-step "ASP" process to move past a prospect's initial reflex resistance.

Step 1—Agreeable Acknowledgement

When you make a prospecting phone call and the prospect quickly gives you resistance, you want to stay as agreeable as you can and acknowledge their position. This will help you lower their defense system and set you up for step two. Here are some examples of agreeable acknowledgements:

- Absolutely
- I totally get it
- I understand completely
- I respect that
- I can see how you feel that way
- Makes sense
- I agree with you
- 100%
- I can see that

You want to have a go-to phrase you like best so you don't have to think about it the next time a prospect gives you reflex resistance. For example, when a FSBO says, "I'm not interested in working with an agent," you could respond with, "I understand and respect that 100%."

Step 2—Strategic Empathy

After you've acknowledged what the prospect has said in a way that puts you both in agreement, you can now use strategic empathy as a pattern interrupt to further lower the prospect's defenses. (Remember, a pattern interrupt breaks an individual's behavioral pattern.)

After your agreeable acknowledgement: "I understand and respect that 100%," you would simply follow that up by saying, "And with this market, you should not need an agent."

This is an example of strategic empathy, of speaking through the prospect's point of view and not your own. The prospect can't believe their ears. They have a real estate agent calling and telling them they don't need an agent to sell their house! This has never happened before and they don't know how to respond other than to be surprised and impressed.

Step 3—Pivot to Another Question Immediately

After showing strategic empathy, the prospect's defense system is rendered almost inoperable, allowing you to move the conversation forward, which is the goal of this three-step process. There should be no pause. I'll repeat, do not pause after showing strategic empathy! If you do, this will not be as effective, as you will have given the prospect a chance to generate more resistance. What you want to do instead is ask another question immediately. When you ask a question, you put them in a position to respond, which ultimately distracts them from their original line of thinking. This is why asking questions is such an important skill in Reverse Selling.

So let's put the whole thing into action so you have an example of how ASP works. Let's pretend you're calling a FSBO.

Prospect: "Thanks for calling but I'm not interested in listing my home with an agent."

Agent: "I totally understand and respect that, and in this market you should not need an agent to sell your home, which was why I was calling to find out, are you open to the idea of an agent at least bringing you a qualified buyer for the home, if it made sense for you?"

So let's review. When you're making prospecting calls, and a prospect naturally gives you reflex resistance, you're going to use the Reverse Selling ASP Method.

A—Agreeable acknowledgement

S—Show strategic empathy

P—Pivot to another question immediately

SKILL #2
USING NON-THREATENING WORDS

There are certain words that, when used, provoke people to become defensive. One of the most common is the word "why?" "Why did you do this?" and "Why did you do that?" come off as accusatory, putting the other person in the defensive role. This is the power of communication. The good news, however, is that Reverse Selling teaches you to use words that do the exact opposite. These words are designed to help you lower a prospect's defenses and actually help the prospect make decisions.

At ReverseSelling.com we refer to these as non-threatening words. You can use them in a variety of situations, such as setting up a follow-up call, scheduling a meeting, or obtaining commitments to do business.

Here's a list of a few of my favorite non-threatening words and some examples of how to use them in action:

- Typically
- Potentially
- Consider
- Interview
- Reasonable
- Unreasonable

Here are some common examples of how to use these words to help you move forward with a prospect.

Example #1: You call a divorce attorney you've been trying to meet with to earn his referral business. When asking for a time to meet, instead of saying, "What day this week works to meet?" you'll simply replace that by saying, "If we did meet one day this week for coffee, what days are typically less busy in the morning?"

Asking, "What day this week works?" puts the prospect on the spot, and most times they will retreat by telling you they will look at their schedule and get back to you. To avoid this from happening, we will get the prospect to agree to a time to meet without them ever feeling threatened or put on the spot.

Example #2: You call a FSBO and they tell you they are not interested in listing with an agent, as they often do. Instead of arguing with them about why they should, simply ask a question using a non-threatening word to identify a potential opportunity. You might say something like, "I understand completely and with this market, chances are you won't need an agent, which is why I'm calling. If by some off chance you don't end up selling on your own in 30 to 60 days from now, which I don't think will happen, would you consider at that point potentially meeting with me to discuss other options?"

This response uses many Reverse Selling skills, removes the perception of threat or accusation, and more often than not elicits a response from the prospect—all because we've created a hypothetical situation that we've convinced them we believe will never happen. This makes it easy for them to surrender information they would otherwise never tell you. Once you have the information you can determine how to proceed with the conversation.

SKILL #3
GIVING THE ILLUSION OF CONTROL

In a sales situation, control has been misunderstood for years. Many people believe the person talking or making demands is the one in control. We use this misunderstanding to our advantage. Chris Voss, the author of *Never Split The Difference*, does a beautiful job of explaining this in his book. Giving the illusion of control means we help comfort a prospect in their decision to meet with us because we create a scenario where they feel 100% in control and one where there's absolutely no threat of being "sold."

Here's an example of what this might sound like. Let's pretend you're calling an expired listing and in your pursuit to set a listing appointment you say, "Let's not agree to anything at this point. Why don't we simply schedule time to meet, and I'll share some information about why the home didn't sell and other options for you to consider that will cause the home to actually sell, and from there, you can decide if working with me in the future makes sense or not. Either way, no big deal. Fair enough?"

Like many of the skills you'll learn in this chapter, there's a combination of skills here but the main takeaway is we are offering to give value to the prospect and removing any potential threat to agree to the meeting when we tell them, "You can decide if working together makes sense or not." This will separate you from every other agent who might be calling them, and makes it clear to them you're coming from a place of contribution vs. high pressure.

SKILL #4
SPEAK IN HYPOTHETICALS ("LET'S PRETEND")

In general, people don't like to be put on the spot. I don't like it either. Many untrained real estate agents make the mistake of putting prospects on the spot by asking, with unapologetic entitlement, very threatening questions and demanding that prospects answer. It's not their fault necessarily—it's what's been taught for years.

I hear agents ask prospects questions like, "Why did you decide to sell FSBO?" This question is setting you up to fail. First of all, asking people questions that start with "Why" almost always requires the other person to defend themselves. Questions like these are asking for a fight with the prospect, which is the last thing you want.

Instead, you want to remove the prospect from their current situation by asking hypothetical questions about future situations and positioning these situations to be very unlikely to happen. We're not tricking the prospect here. We cannot see into the future and neither can the prospect. We are simply asking questions about situations that, in our experience, could potentially arise.

As an example, you may or may not know but the majority of FSBOs will end up listing their home with an agent somewhere between four to eight weeks in the future if they can't sell it on their own. Now, the interesting thing is that when speaking with someone selling FSBO, they believe with every fiber of their being that they don't want to work with an agent—and won't have to. This is simply inexperienced optimism. So instead of arguing with a FSBO about why they should use an agent, potentially losing out on the opportunity altogether, all we need to do is ask about a hypothetical situation in the future that the prospect believes will never happen.

For example, we simply ask the FSBO, "In this market, chances are you won't need an agent to help you sell your home, which is why I'm curious, if by some off chance you can't sell the home in 30, 60, 90 days from now, at that point, would you consider looking into some other options to get the home sold?"

The prospect is willing to answer because their optimism is high at this point. They think to themselves that the hypothetical situation you've described will never happen, and so therefore there's no harm in answering your question and in giving you information. This is the power of this skill. The FSBO then says, with a little sarcasm in their voice, "I don't think that will happen but sure, if I haven't sold the house by then I'd be open to looking at some other options."

This is exactly what you're looking for! You've now identified a future listing opportunity that none of your competitors had the skill to uncover.

SKILL #5
BE GENUINELY CURIOUS

When you can come across as being genuinely curious on a prospecting call, it's more likely that the prospect will open up. For example, when calling an expired listing, you want to communicate as though you're in disbelief that the home didn't sell and you're calling to understand what happened. This furthers the prospect's illusion of control, which is what they want. Think about it. How do you feel when someone asks you for advice or asks for your opinion on something? It almost feels as though you have instant power over that person, as if you know something they do not. Be genuinely curious and you'll get the prospect to talk and open up.

SKILL #6
BE A CHAMELEON

Every prospect is different and has unique personality traits. This requires you to adjust how you communicate accordingly. There are four main personality styles you must understand deeply to become a master salesperson: the Driver, the Expressive, the Amiable, and the Analytical. First, you must understand yourself by becoming self-aware. Tony Robbins has a free personality assessment on his website that you should take now. Go to www.tonyrobbins.com/disc/. If you've never taken a personality assessment, this will be an eye-opening activity for you. Being self-aware is extremely valuable, and it will allow you to adapt to any personality style like a chameleon.

Let's start off with the Driver, since they are the ones who are least patient. A Driver personality is the person who takes charge, wants results, and wants to get right to the point. Drivers can come across as very dominant and direct with their demands.

Communicating with Drivers

When communicating with a Driver, avoid giving too much information and get right to the point. Be sure you don't take what the Driver says personally or get emotional. Drivers have very little regard for your feelings.

If you're an Expressive personality, avoid talking too much and going on tangents. If you're an Analytical, be careful: Drivers are easily annoyed by Analyticals. Stay away from the details and focus on the end result. For Amiables, you're in luck: Drivers generally like Amiables because they are good listeners and do what the Driver says without questioning it. If you're an Amiable, just make sure to be confident when you do need to talk.

Communicating with Expressives

Expressives love to talk and thrive on recognition and personal compliments. They are the life of the party and are excited about everything. When communicating with Expressives, focus on the relationship, show excitement, and give praise.

If you're a Driver communicating with a prospect who is an Expressive, you'll likely want to tell them to shut up at some point. Don't! Be patient and listen, which will be hard for you to do. You'll want to cut them off, but again, don't—just let them talk. If you're an Analytical, be careful not to bore the prospect. Keep things moving and ask them a lot of questions. Amiables and Expressives tend to get along quite well since they both thrive on their emotions.

Communicating with Amiables

Amiables tend to get along with everyone and are easy to like as they aim to please others. Amiables want to know that you care and when they do, they will be one of your best clients. For the Drivers, be careful not to dominate the entire conversation because the Amiable will let you. Be sure to include them from time to time by getting their point of view. For Analyticals, be sure to focus on the human connection, as well as on the facts and figures. Expressives find it easy to communicate with Amiables, as they are able to connect with ease.

Communicating with Analyticals

This is the hard one for salespeople and real estate agents. Analyticals are the engineer-types who obsess over the details. Analyticals tend to take a very long time to make decisions so be careful not to pressure them to make a decision too soon.

Drivers, this is your biggest challenge. Be sure to present as much information as you can and as hard as it is for you, be patient. If you try to bulldoze your way into a sale, it will be over. Analyticals don't deal well with confrontation and you'll lose a client forever. Analyticals are not too fond of Expressives, so be sure to take it down a notch or two if you're Expressive. Don't be so animated and enthusiastic, but rather go slow and be more methodical in your communication. For Amiables, it's easy for you to get along with Analyticals—just be sure you don't get too mushy, and be sure to communicate the facts and figures in great detail.

SKILL #7
USE THE F-WORD

I'm not talking about that F-word—I'm talking about the word "fair." Fair is probably one of the most powerful and effective words you have as a real estate agent. Being treated fairly is the number one way to remove a prospect's feeling of being threatened. People find it safe to communicate in situations where they believe they will be treated fairly and without pressure.

HOW TO USE THE F-WORD IN YOUR SALES APPROACH

Anytime you ask a prospect for any type of commitment, whether regarding a follow-up call, a meeting, or asking for the business, you'll want to strategically use the F-word to gain their agreement.

Here's an example. Let's pretend you're calling an absentee owner and your goal is to set a preview appointment. You'll combine Skill 2, "Using Non-threatening Words," and Skill 3, "Giving the Illusion of Control," and then end with Skill 7, "Using the F-word," to gain agreement. It might sound like this: "Mr. Prospect, let's do this. Why don't we meet at the house one day so I can take a look, and while I'm there, I'll share how much the home would sell for in today's market and then you can decide if selling now makes sense or not, fair enough?" The prospect can't help but to agree because what you've laid out is in fact very fair, and you've positioned the meeting in such a way where any and all threat of being sold has been removed.

SKILL #8
ASK SOCRATIC-STYLE QUESTIONS

Socratic-style questioning, also referred to as the Socratic Method, is a dialogue between two people where one person asks open-ended questions to help the other party arrive at logical conclusions via a process of rational analysis. In Reverse Selling, we use Socratic-style questions to help prospects arrive at their own conclusions and truths without having to tell them. No one wants to be told anything, but if it's their own idea, it becomes their reality.

Here's an example. Let's say you're talking with a potential seller about the price of their home and a strategy to get the home sold. Instead of you doing all the talking and telling, which goes against Reverse Selling Rule #19—"If You're Telling, You're Not Selling," you'll ask questions that lead the seller to their own logical conclusion. It might sound like this: "Mrs. Seller, homes in your neighborhood sell extremely fast, and in some cases with multiple offers. If your home ends up sitting on the market for a long time, what do we run the risk of?" We want the seller to tell us using their words that sitting on the market is bad, and if we do, it's because the price of the home is too high.

We also want the seller to tell us that we should lower the price at certain times in the process without us having to nag the seller for a price adjustment. If you've been selling real estate for any length of time, you know it's nearly impossible to tell a seller their house is overpriced without some type of argument. So get the seller to tell you by asking Socratic-style questions.

Let's finish the sample conversation:

Prospect: "If the home sits on the market for too long, people might start giving us lowball offers."

Agent: "I agree, and so if for some reason we hit the market, and in two or three weeks we haven't received an offer, what do you believe we need to do immediately?"

Prospect: "At that point, we probably need to lower the price."

Agent: "Yes, I would agree."

Imagine a world where you never have to argue with a seller again about the price of their home. Master asking Socratic-style questions and this will be your reality.

SKILL #9
SPEAK THROUGH THE PROSPECT'S POINT OF VIEW, NOT YOURS

We've talked a lot in this book about connecting with prospects, lowering their defenses, and showing them we care. Nothing does this better than speaking through the prospect's point of view rather than our own. For example, if you're speaking with an expired listing and they tell you they are no longer selling, which most sellers with expired listings will, you can respond with, "Makes total sense, and if I was you, I might want to take a break from the market and review all my options too." Doing this is another example of a pattern interrupt and will help to lower the prospect's defenses, allowing you to ask another question on your prospecting call. We also call this strategic empathy.

SKILL #10
BE AGREEABLE

The issue with most selling techniques is they lead us to challenging the prospect's point of view, which in most cases ends in an argument. If you're going to get anywhere in a sales conversation with a prospect, you must always stay agreeable and never break Rule #10, which is Never Argue With a Prospect. This doesn't mean you need to agree with the prospect, but be agreeable so you are able to move the conversation forward. For example, if a prospect tells you they want to wait until spring to sell their home, rather than argue why they shouldn't, simply respond with, "I can understand that." This will allow you to ask the prospect another question or give them more information that may change their mind.

SKILL #11
GAINING AGREEMENT

Gauging a prospect's level of interest at critical times in the prospecting call or sales meeting is vital to your success. Many times you'll get to the end of a prospecting call or listing appointment and the prospect will say, "Let me think about it and I'll get back with you." This means two things. One, the prospect has no interest but just didn't have the guts to tell you, and two, you never gauged the prospect's interest level by engaging them into the process. Gaining agreement will help you do just that.

Here's an example:

Let's pretend you're on a prospecting call and you're talking with a potential seller, trying to schedule a listing appointment. Rather than using high pressure tactics to set the appointment (like traditional selling techniques teach) just to have the prospect cancel at a later time, you instead engage the prospect to ensure the listing appointment does in fact make sense for them by gaining their agreement along the way. It might sound like this: "Mr. Seller, when we meet, we can discuss a pricing strategy that will cause your home to actually sell so you end up netting the money you need in your pocket bottom line. Does that sound reasonable?"

You want to pay close attention to their response. If they respond with a firm, "Yes, that makes sense," that's a good sign. We never want to force leads or appointments. Instead, we need to engage the prospect at every point to ensure everyone is on the same page. Use this skill as a checkpoint in your sales process. If you gain agreement and the prospect is in alignment, keep moving forward. If not, you know where you need to spend a little more time.

SKILL #12
MASTER THE ART OF SILENCE

When you ask a prospect a question, shut up and listen to the answer. Too many untrained real estate agents talk too much and worse, after they finally do get around to asking a question (which is the goal of selling), they cut the prospect off, finish their sentences, and just keep putting their foot in their mouth. Let the prospect carry the weight of their pain. Don't let them off the hook! When you ask a question about their situation or desired outcome, let them answer. The goal is to keep them talking. Once you've mastered the art of silence, you'll start to have prospects asking you how they can do business with you. The one listening is the one who holds the power.

SKILL #13
UPSWINGS AND DOWNSWINGS

Upswings and downswings describe how we use our tonality when delivering a question or statement. Generally speaking, upswings should be used for questions while downswings should be used for statements. When using an upswing to ask a question, your tone of voice should go up at the end of the question so the delivery is more inviting for the prospect to answer. When using downswings for statements, the opposite should happen. When you make a statement, the tone of your voice should go down, sounding matter of fact and confident.

SKILL #14
FORESHADOWING

Think back to the last time you went to a haunted house. I don't care how tough you are, everyone feels a level of discomfort and anxiety. Why? Because of the unknown. What if before you went into the haunted house, your friend told you what to expect at every turn and as you walked into the haunted house, all the lights were on? Would you be scared? Of course not! The haunted house business would be gone. The haunted house industry brings in over $500 million a year because of its ability to keep people in the dark and in the unknown. If you're going to be a great real estate agent, you'll need to make a living doing the exact opposite. Part of your job is to lower your prospect's anxiety by explaining exactly what they can expect at every step of the process. You'll use this skill when you're setting appointments, before a listing appointment, and when you take a listing.

Here's an example of a foreshadow at a listing appointment. At the beginning of the meeting when both you and the prospect are a little tense, you'll use a foreshadow to help lower the prospect's anxiety. Here's what it might sound like: "Mr. and Mrs. Seller, thanks again for the opportunity to earn your business. I'm going to ask you a few questions to ensure we're on the same page, then I'll walk you through how I plan to get your home sold and give you an idea of how much money you can expect to walk away with from the sale. From there, we can decide if working together makes sense or not. Does that seem fair?"

This lays out exactly how the meeting will go so that the seller knows what to expect. When you've mastered the ability to foreshadow, you'll find yourself closing more business than you ever have before, and it will be because you've learned how to make people feel confident and comfortable.

SKILL #15
USING ASSUMPTIVE LANGUAGE

There will be times you'll need to confidently move the process forward to help the prospect get what they want. Now let me be clear: There's a massive difference between being assumptive and being pushy. With the Reverse Selling Method, using assumptive language allows us to get to the point to ask for what we want while removing resistance and threat from the prospect at the same time. Being pushy is where you force a prospect to make a yes-or-no decision on the spot, like a take-it-or-leave-it type of mentality. You'll need to learn how to use assumptive language to help bridge the gap between conversations with prospects and getting the prospects to make decisions. Here are some examples of assumptive statements you'll use in combination with other Reverse Selling skills.

- "Let's do this."
- "Let's not agree to anything right now."
- "Here's what we'll do."
- "Why don't we do this."

Here's an example of how you might use assumptive language in action: Let's pretend you call a FSBO and try everything you know how to do to set an appointment but the prospect is just not having it. You'll learn more about something called the prospecting waterfall in a later chapter, but for now, since you can't get the appointment, your next goal is to generate a lead for your seller lead database and start following up to play the long game. So here's what you say: "Mrs. Prospect, I understand it might not make sense to meet now. Let's do this: I'll email you a copy of my FSBO backup plan. Take a look at it and if it's something you'd like to discuss in the future, we can do that. Does that sound fair?"

Your goal here is to capture the prospect's email address and live to call another day. When the prospect agrees to this and provides you with their email, the prospect treats this as a win because they have successfully rejected your attempt at scheduling a meeting. This is exactly why using assumptive language works so well. You were able to generate a lead, provide the prospect with valuable information, and establish a good lead to follow up with in the future. And when you do, you'll stand out from all the other agents calling, because unlike every other agent you've been able to get your information into their hands, creating more context for future follow up.

SKILL #16
SETTING APPOINTMENTS

Never forget the purpose of a prospecting call is to set an appointment. To successfully become an appointment-setting machine, you must learn how to combine many of the Reverse Selling skills and understand them intimately. Here are the skills you'll combine to make setting appointments with prospects easy. Yes, that's not a typo. When you combine these skills, setting face-to-face appointments and listing appointments will be easy.

Skills used in combination to set appointments:

1. Skill #2—Use Non-threatening Words
2. Skill #3—Giving the Illusion of Control
3. Skill #7—Use The F-word
4. Skill #11—Gaining Agreement
5. Skill #15—Use Assumptive Language

Here's an example of how you'll combine these five skills to successfully set appointments. Let's say you're calling an expired listing with the intention to set a listing appointment. You've gone through some discovery early on in the call (which you'll learn more about when we get to scripts) and now it's time for you to ask for what you want, which is an appointment.

Here's what it might sound like:

"Mrs. Prospect, let's not agree to anything over the phone. Let's simply schedule time to meet one day this week so we can review a plan that will cause your home to actually sell. And then after we've had a chance to meet, you can decide if working with me might make sense for you or not. Either way, no big deal—does that seem fair?"

Let's break this down. We start this process off by using the prospect's first name, which to them is the most beautiful word in the English language. This captures their attention the same way it did for you when your teacher called out your name in school. Then we say, "Let's not agree to anything over the phone," which is designed to remove any and all pressure the prospect may be feeling. We then move on using assumptive language by saying, "Let's simply schedule time to meet one day this week, so we can review a plan that will cause your home to actually sell." This provides the prospect with what they want, which is to sell their home and therefore, they see value in the meeting. We then continue to remove the threat in meeting by giving the prospect the illusion of control, saying, "And then after we've had a chance to meet, you can decide if working with me might make sense for you or not. Either way, no big deal." Then we use the F-word to get the prospect to agree to the meeting saying, "Does that seem fair?"

This type of communication is not what the prospect has grown accustomed to hearing from real estate agents and it helps them feel a sense of comfort in their decision to meet with you. In some cases, they may even tell you how much they appreciate how different your approach is—depending upon their personality type, of course.

There are many different script variations you can combine to create a successful Reverse Selling appointment-setting strategy. Be sure to take time to write out your appointment-setting script and master it. I'll teach you how to do this when we talk about scripts.

SKILL #17
RESPONDING TO OBJECTIONS

OK, now it's time to talk about everyone's favorite topic—objections, and how to handle them. By far, the most common question I get from agents in my coaching program is, "What should I say when the prospect says this?" First things first.

Unlike what is commonly taught by the "gurus," you cannot overcome objections! There are no magic words you can say that will change a person's entire belief system in a matter of seconds. If there were, I'd know about it. Not to mention that if this was possible, all of the fighting over political and religious differences would be history, an achievement that does not seem to be happening any time soon. However, it is possible to effectively respond to a prospect's objection in a way that allows you to keep the conversation and process moving forward, which is the goal.

In this section, I'll teach you the five-step process for responding to any objection or resistance that you'll ever get. And yes, when we get to scripts, I'll get you the actual words to say verbatim. But for now let's just focus on understanding these concepts. By the way, these concepts work great in a real estate sales capacity, and also in any situation in life where there's potential for conflict or opposing viewpoints.

Step 1—Agreeable Acknowledgement

If you're going to have success with responding to objections, you can never become defensive, never argue, and must be agreeable at all times. The moment you lose control of your emotions, you're done. In step one, you simply want to respond with an agreeable acknowledgement without hesitation. This will show the prospect you're listening to what they are saying, and more importantly, that you respect their point of view. This step might be the most important one of the five, because without it, you're asking for an argument.

Here are some examples of agreeable acknowledgements we use in the Reverse Selling Method:

- Absolutely
- I totally get it
- I understand completely
- I respect that
- I can see how you feel that way
- Makes sense
- I agree with you
- 100%
- I can see that

Step 2—Strategic Empathy

It's very powerful when someone believes you truly understand their point of view and where they are coming from. In step 2, this is exactly what we're doing. With whatever objection you receive, you'll want to speak through the prospect's point of view and not your own.

Here's an example. If a FSBO tells you they are not interested in listing with an agent, step 2 of this process (strategic empathy) would sound like this: "Mr. Prospect, if I was you, I wouldn't want to hire an agent either, especially in a seller's market like this."

This also serves as a pattern interrupt, which is why step 2 is so powerful. If you've been prospecting for any length of time, you know you're not the only real estate agent calling these leads. The prospect is not used to an agent speaking this way—being so agreeable and taking their side. It throws them off. They are used to agents calling and arguing with them, trying to convince them that to sell FSBO is a bad idea and that working with an agent is so much better.

Step 3—Use an Assumptive Statement

If you've successfully executed the first two steps, you've put yourself in a position to move the conversation forward. At this point, the prospect is a little stunned and even surprisingly impressed. Now is the time to suggest a potential next step with absolute conviction and confidence. You've earned the prospect's respect at this point, so if done correctly, the prospect will now hear you out like you've done with them. The particular assumptive statement you use depends upon which outcome you are looking to achieve. For example, if your goal is to set an appointment with the prospect, you might say something like, "Mrs. Prospect, let's not agree to anything over the phone. Let's simply schedule time to meet one day this week."

Step 4—Use a Value Statement

Your goal in step 4 is to sell the value of the appointment. In other words, your value statement must answer this question: Why would the prospect want to meet with you? As you're creating your go-to script, you'll want to think about the most likely desired outcome of the prospect and use that in your value statement. For example, what do sellers want when their listing expires? That's right—to get their home sold. What about someone who is selling their home while going through the probate process? They most likely need help getting the house cleaned up and ready to sell. So depending on what lead sources you're calling, your value statement should reflect what they most likely want.

Here's an example the agents in our coaching program often use: "Mr. Prospect, when we meet, I'll review a plan that will cause your home to sell for a premium so you'll net the most money possible in your pocket, bottom line."

Step 5—Gain Agreement by Giving the Illusion of Control

In this last step, you'll combine two skills to move the conversation forward. You'll give the prospect the illusion of control to help lower any perceived threat, and then gain agreement by using the F-word. It might sound like this, "And then after we've had a chance to meet, you can decide if working with me might make sense for you or not. Either way no big deal, fair enough?"

Now let's put it all together so you can see how this process works in action. This is just one example. The next time an expired listing tells you that they are going to "list the house with the same agent," which is another very common objection you'll get when prospecting expired listings, you'll respond using this five-step process:

Prospect: "Thanks for calling but we're going to relist the home with the same agent."

Reverse Selling Trained Agent: "I understand and if I was you, I'd probably feel comfortable doing the same thing too. Let's do this. Obviously you're not going to do anything unless it makes sense so let's meet and I'll share a new strategy with you that will cause your home to actually sell. And after we've had a chance to meet, you'll at least have another agent's opinion and you can then decide if working with me or continuing to work with your previous agent still makes sense. Does that seem fair and reasonable?"

SKILL #18
REVERSE CLOSING

For years, the real estate sales industry has made closing the main focus. "Close, close, close," is all you've heard for years. Making matters worse, countless Hollywood movies have perpetuated and amplified the perception of closing to be the main skill of selling. Here's the truth: It is not! Yes, asking for the business is critical to obtaining new business. There's no doubt, however, closing the sale has very little to do with what happens at the end of the sales presentation. If a salesperson has a problem closing new business, it's because everything they did leading up to asking for the business was done incorrectly. In other words, if you have a problem closing, it's most likely you have a problem opening. Reverse Closing should be a simple process that you and the prospect find easy and mutually beneficial. Closing, according to traditional selling methodology, has been taught to be a process of applying pressure to a prospect to make a decision, and you keep applying more pressure until they buy or until you lose the relationship forever, whichever comes first.

Reverse Closing is when you get the prospect to pull from you next steps versus you having to push the prospect to the next step. Imagine two magnets facing opposite sides. What happens when you try to push them together? This is an example of old traditional closing techniques. With Reverse Closing, the exact opposite should occur. If you've done everything correctly leading up to the time when you and the prospect will decide whether or not to do business together, it should be like two magnets that, when let go, come together automatically without friction or any resistance.

The goal of Reverse Closing is to ask specific questions in such a way that the prospect will close themselves. I know—that's a big promise, but it's true. Here's how it works.

Assuming you've done everything correctly up to this point, you can simply say to the prospect, "Mr. and Mrs. Prospect, based on our conversations, I feel confident I can absolutely get your home sold and I'm curious, would you feel comfortable with me as your agent if we did end up working together?"

Now, this is a very neutral question because we're not asking for the prospect to commit, nor are they committing to anything when they answer. This is why the majority of your prospects, when asked correctly, will say, "Yes, we feel comfortable with you."

Now from this point, the prospect has told us with their own words that they are comfortable with us. If they weren't, they'd give you some type of objection right here. Next, we want to find out if they are in agreement with the most important things every seller cares about most, which are the numbers: How much you're going to sell their home for, and how much they can expect to walk away with. And because you've already gained their agreement earlier in the process on the price of the home and the cost of selling, there should be no reason for any hesitation here. So you'll simply respond to the prospect with, "Great, and with everything we've discussed to get your home sold and after looking at all the numbers, is this something you feel will work for you?"

If the prospect responds positively, we can go to the final step and say, "Well, if you thought it made sense to move forward, we can quickly get some paperwork completed and I could get started by scheduling our photographer. Is there anything else you'd like to discuss or should we get started?"

Now, when you can give up old habits of trying to "close" the prospect, and you give the perceived control right back to the consumer, you'll be amazed at how the prospect responds. And because they've never dealt with a real estate agent like you before, they are taken aback once again and start to view you more as their trusted advisor; they can't help but want to work with you. You're like the magnet pulling them closer vs. pushing like all other untrained agents tend to do. This is the power of Reverse Closing.

6 | Why Face-to-Face Meetings Change Everything

Have you ever had one of those really difficult mornings where nothing seems to go smoothly? Of course you have. You can feel it in the pit of your stomach—the day's about to turn sour. You finally make it to work and try to forget your morning by focusing on your work, when all of a sudden someone says to you, "Geez, did someone wake up on the wrong side of the bed this morning?" You didn't even say a word to them! You didn't have to.

In the field of psychology there is a concept known as emotional contagion, which describes the emotional transference that occurs between humans in the context of social interactions in close proximity. It doesn't tend to occur in remote interactions where only verbal and even visual cues are exchanged. This means human beings, and other animals for that matter, have the ability to detect non-verbal cues when in proximity to others that lets them know critical data about the emotional state of those around them. This is when your co-workers can usually tell when you've had a rough morning. This also means that in remote interactions, such as phone or video calls, the phenomenon known as emotional contagion does not tend to occur.

"So, what does this have to do with real estate," you ask? Everything! When it comes to converting leads into listings, a face-to-face meeting changes everything! When you're talking with a prospect on the phone, no matter how good your skills are, you won't be able to convey the subtle non-verbal and emotional cues that will make the prospect feel comfortable with you. To them, you are little more than a stranger—you must never forget this. Unless you're talking in person they may not feel comfortable, and so they do not give you access to their true motivations. In addition, you will not be able to read whether the prospect is tracking with you emotionally as you present your case over the phone. This may result in a lost opportunity if you read the prospect wrong.

If, however, by using the Reverse Selling Method and skills outlined in this book, you shift your focus slightly from closing deals over the phone, to just getting face to face with the prospect, you will find that the prospect will feel much more comfortable communicating with you in person. This is when your prospects are the most likely to open up to you, and when you can really begin to build a relationship with them. This is where they are most likely to uncover opportunities that might arise for you to help them with their real estate needs. This is where you can really start to be of service and establish yourself as a real asset in your market.

To be clear, we define a face-to-face meeting as a meeting between you and a homeowner who is thinking about selling their home, without any expectations of working together at this moment. The meeting was set up and agreed to by the prospect with the understanding that you'd preview their home and give them information that could potentially help them to get their property sold now or in the future.

For years, I took the advice thousands of other real estate agents around the world also take from these "gurus" who tell us to prequalify 100% before you go out on an appointment. Now, conceptually this advice makes sense. Of course you'd prefer to only leave your office or home office to go on appointments where the consumer tells you upfront they are ready to do business with you. But unfortunately, this is just not how it works in the real world. Yes, when hearing this from the guru on stage at a conference, you can certainly rationalize this theory, but here's the truth: Even the agents who swear by the teachings of these famous real estate coaching gurus don't follow their advice on a consistent basis. I know. I was one of them.

Along my journey in the real estate business, I've been fortunate enough to have masterminded with some of the industry's biggest producers—agents earning more than $1 million per year in personal net income selling houses. And the interesting thing is, while rarely would any of these agents ever challenge these gurus in public on this advice, behind closed doors they do not prequalify most of their appointments. In this chapter, you'll learn why we at ReverseSelling.com make such a big deal out of getting face-to-face meetings.

There are two major flaws in the advice being given to agents regarding never going to an appointment without prequalifying. The first is a simple misunderstanding of human behavior. I referenced this example earlier in the book, but let's take a closer look at it now: If you're married, have a boyfriend, girlfriend, or have ever had a relationship with another person, you'll most likely agree that the relationship developed over time. It's rare, if ever, that two people meet for the very first time, and at that first meeting decide to get married. However, this is the advice the "gurus" want you to take. They suggest that we prospect and call strangers out of the blue, and within just a few minutes of talking on the phone for the first time, try to convince them to do business with us immediately. Oh, and if they don't agree, don't go on the appointment, throw away the number and move on to the next lead. Are you kidding me? How these gurus don't get sued for malpractice giving this advice is a mystery that I cannot understand.

If that isn't enough, think about this: Why would a complete stranger commit to doing business with you after only spending a few minutes on a random phone call? I know, it's crazy—most people won't. And not only will they not commit to doing business with you right on the spot, but it's also very unlikely that they will give you any real information about their situation.

We're salespeople the consumers do not trust. They have no incentive to give us information over the phone. They say what is necessary to get you off the phone as quickly as possible without being rude. Some people aren't worried about being rude and are quick to hang up on your ass or even worse, give you an earful. This is why this advice is ludicrous and why it makes more sense to shift your approach and focus on getting face to face, or at least to a Zoom meeting as it's happening these days.

Most people are much more willing to open up once they feel comfortable with you. This is exactly what a face-to-face meeting does. Let me explain: For years, I'd call FSBOs, and of course, most of the time they would tell me they are not interested in working with an agent. I would then try to take the advice so many real estate gurus give and try to convince them that they should use an agent. Then they would hang up on me. And this would repeat, call after call, day after day. And to make matters worse, just days after hearing from the FSBO they were not interested in working with an agent, I would see their house listed with a competitor! "How can this be?" I used to ask myself. "Surely, it's me," I used to think. But it wasn't. It was bad advice and a bad approach that I was taught, just like so many others.

After thousands of calls, and failing over and over, I'd had enough. I remember telling myself, "There's something missing. I talk to a FSBO one day and they tell me they are not interested in listing with a real estate agent, and the next day, they are listed with a real estate agent!" I was done trying to convince the prospect over the phone that they were wrong and why my way was better. I was done trying to qualify every lead because there was rarely ever a lead that qualified under the definition I was being taught. I said, "You know what? When I'm in front of a prospect, I do great. I'm just going to focus on getting in front of these prospects and see what happens." And wow, did this open my eyes! I didn't worry when a FSBO told me they weren't interested or when an expired listing said they were no longer selling, I went on the appointment anyway. This later become known as Rule #1 in the Reverse Selling Method, Nothing Is As It Seems.

What happened on these appointments was nothing less than amazing. The FSBO who told me over the phone that they would never list their house with a Realtor was now meeting with me at their kitchen table and asking me about my services! The expired listing who told me on the phone they decided not to sell was now having coffee with me and asking me what I could do to get their property sold. I couldn't believe it! At first, I was mad. Not at the prospect but with the gurus who gave me such bad advice, and at myself for listening to them for so long. The amount of money I lost in commissions is unfathomable. Then I cried—seriously. I remember leaving a FSBO preview appointment that went so well, that on my way back to the office I pulled off to the side of the road, got out of my car, and cried. They were tears of joy. I was overcome with excitement that I had found an approach that was so powerful and so effective and that none of my competitors knew about at the time! I figured out how to get in front of motivated sellers where my competitors could not, and I learned how to discover new listings where the competition saw none. The next full year, I was able to list and sell over 100 homes using this method you now know as Reverse Selling.

The second major flaw with regard to this advice is that it violates something called the law of large numbers. In probability theory, the law of large numbers suggests that the average of results obtained through consistent repetition will hold true as you continue to repeat it. In other words, when an action is performed consistently over time, it will produce a predictable result. For example, let's take the game of roulette. This game is played at casinos around the world. Although a casino may lose money on a spin here or there, over time it's a statistical probability that the casino will come out ahead because your odds of winning are 37 to 1, no matter how many spins or how long you play.

Here's how this works in real estate and the same is true with prospecting. After years of tracking and comparing the prospecting numbers of agents around the world with my own numbers, I discovered that it takes an average of about 100 actual conversations with homeowners to find one "qualified" appointment (as defined by the gurus). It only takes about five conversations to schedule a face-to-face appointment. You with me so far? Now we have to look at a few more averages. We have to see not what people say they do, or what they say they're going to do when they're all excited and building their business plan, but what they actually do. The truth is, most real estate agents don't prospect.

Don't believe me? Go to your office tomorrow and ask every single agent if they prospected today. Exactly. You're probably laughing because you know what the answer will be. But when averaged across the span of a year, those agents who do only prospect for about 30 minutes per day.

On average, if an agent uses some type of auto-dialer, they will talk to about 10 people per hour. If an agent takes the same bad advice I did and buys into the idea of over-qualifying every lead, it will take them about a month of prospecting daily to find one "qualified" appointment. Why? Because it takes 100 conversations to set one qualified appointment. At 10 conversations per hour, (five conversations per day as a result of 30 minutes of prospecting) this equals one opportunity per month. Let's go even further. On average, agents have a 50% conversion ratio at a listing appointment, meaning they will get five listings for every 10 listing appointments they attend. In this case, the agent who follows this method will set 12 appointments for the year and most likely get six listings and sell four. Four homes sold for the year!

We haven't even talked about the problem yet! Remember the law of large numbers and probability theory? Is it probable (notice I didn't say possible, I said probable) that you or any other agent is going to continue prospecting, getting rejected and beat up on the phone every day for these types of results? No! That's the other problem with this advice. You could make the argument and say, "Yeah, but Brandon, what if an agent made 100 contacts a day? They would set one qualified appointment every day." Right. And I would respond with, "How likely is that?" Find me a real estate agent who prospects every single day for 10 hours a day—remember, 10 contacts per hour.

Now, on the other hand, I think you'd agree that it is in fact likely that because of the law of averages, you can manage to prospect for a minimum of 30 minutes a day. With 30 minutes a day, it's likely that you'd actually speak with five prospects. And yet again, because of the law of averages and the law of large numbers, it's a statistical probability that you'd set one face-to-face appointment every day! Now, let me ask you this: Is it probable that if you set an appointment every single day, you'd be excited about your business? Be excited to do it again and again? Of course! So, what would happen to your business if you worked five days a week and were face to face with 20 motivated sellers every month? Do you think you'd get listings? Absolutely! You'll learn more about these ratios later. But for now, suffice it to say that there is just too much upside to be gained not to be focused on setting face-to-face appointments, while the downsides or risks associated with focusing only on what the gurus call "qualified appointments" is just too great. Do you see now the value of the face-to-face appointment? Have I beat on this point enough? I hope so because here's the truth: A face-to-face meeting changes everything.

7 | Lead Generation

PROSPECTING IS NOT COLD-CALLING

There's a process in nature called natural selection by which organisms better adapted to their environment tend to survive and reproduce more than those less adapted to their environment. For example, let's explore the process by which a lioness hunts her prey. As the herd of antelope crosses a river, the lioness does not attack immediately, aimlessly running into the river chasing hundreds of antelope. No, she waits patiently, allowing the process of natural selection to take its course. The lioness, being the fierce predator she is, knows what she is doing. She waits until she spots the weakest link. This is the antelope struggling to get across the river. Then she acts. Without hesitation and with absolute ferocity, she successfully captures her dinner.

Prospecting is not cold-calling for this same reason. Cold-calling would be like the lions chasing all of the antelope into the river and catching none. Prospecting is more like the lioness who, using a process akin to natural selection, carefully selects her prey based upon what she knows will increase her likelihood of achieving success. Let me explain. Cold-calling is picking up the phone and calling random people without any evidence that these people have a need to sell their home. Can it work? Sure, if you're committed to countless hours on the phone, searching for that needle in a haystack. But as I mentioned in Chapter 6, the probability of this happening consistently is very low. Prospecting on the other hand, is strategic. It's a carefully planned activity where we call a targeted group of people where we already have concrete evidence that the likelihood of their need to sell is high. Do you get it? If you had the choice to call 10 homeowners that you knew with 100% certainty were selling their home or 10 random homeowners, which would you choose? Exactly my point.

THE FOUR LEAD GENERATION PILLARS

Have you ever tried sitting in a chair that has less than four legs? It doesn't end well, and in some cases, it ends in disaster. Well, the same thing happens with most real estate agents. Most agents I coach have only one lead generation pillar in their business, and in many cases it's their friends and family or sphere-of-influence. Like the chair with less than four legs, agents who have less than four pillars or lead generation sources also end in disaster more often than not. By "disaster" I mean failing out of the business! Here are the four lead-generation pillars every agent should have as a part of their business plan:

1. The Big Three Hand-Raisers
2. Specialty Niches
3. Referral Partners
4. Sphere of Influence

PILLAR 1 – THE BIG THREE HAND-RAISERS

There are three lead sources that every real estate agent should have in their business plan, and should be working to master: Expired Listings, For Sale by Owners (or FSBOs), and For Rent by Owners (also known as FRBOs). Two arguments I always hear from agents about why they aren't working these sources are 1) they are very competitive and 2) there are not that many to work.

Both of these arguments have some truth to them, but if you look at the top producers across all of North America, you'll find that they all have mastered these three lead sources, and that these sources make up about 20% to 30% of their business. For an agent selling 80 to 100 homes a year, that's a lot of business.

You'll also find the agents with the highest skill will reap most of the reward and will convert the majority of these leads into listings. So, if you have any thoughts of becoming a top producer, you'll need to master these three lead sources.

I always respond to the two arguments by presenting the two massive upsides to working these sources of business. One upside is that these sources of business offer something no other source of business can, which is that we know with 100% certainty these homeowners have a need to sell their home. If you're new to lead generation, this is often the hardest part—knowing where to spend your time, energy, effort, and resources. Well, just like the process of natural selection in nature, we in the real estate business have this same benefit. These three lead sources are the lowest hanging fruit in this business.

The other massive upside to working these sources is that they are the quickest way to generate new business and income for yourself. If you're like me, you need a way to generate business and income today. Yes, future income is great, but we need to eat today.

Another common question I get from agents is, "What is the fastest way to generate new business and get listings?" The answer: Expired listings, FSBOs, and FRBOs. No other lead source has a faster conversion opportunity than these because these homeowners have already decided to sell!

Let's take a deeper look into these three lead sources, and how you can start to succeed by working them.

EXPIRED LISTINGS

Expired listings are probably the lowest of the low-hanging fruit, but certainly the most competitive. Here's why. An expired listing gives us, the real estate agent, great insight about the homeowner. It's literally like most of the work has been done for us. For example, there's absolutely no debate—we know this homeowner wants to move. Second, we also know they are willing to hire a real estate agent and pay a commission. Third, we now know what price for the home won't work, thus making pricing this home easy. This is why so many agents love working expired listings. Pricing property is difficult, and when a home doesn't sell, it's mainly because it was priced too high, making it easier to come up with the right price. Fourth is something most agents don't think about, which is that with an expired listing, you have a seller who has already been through the ringer, most likely with a bad agent—an agent who was not willing to tell them the truth and an agent who was ultimately not able to sell their home. If you do your job correctly, you'll have a client for life. And in some cases, expired listings are the easiest homes to sell the second time around.

With all of this comes fierce competition. As mentioned before, expired listings are the lowest hanging fruit by far, thus producing the fastest opportunity to generate income for agents. This means, of course, the best agents in town will be going after these leads. So to have success when prospecting expired listings, here are a few things to focus on:

1. Be the first voice. If you can be the first one to talk to a homeowner after their home failed to sell, the better off the conversation will go and it's more likely you will be able to set a face-to-face meeting on that first call. By noon, that poor homeowner will receive hundreds of calls from agents.

2. You want to really utilize Reverse Selling Skill #5—Be Genuinely Curious. When speaking with someone whose home did not sell, you want to communicate as if you're a detective trying to figure out what happened. This will help to lower the prospect's defenses and get them talking.

FOR SALE BY OWNERS (FSBOS)

FSBOs are one of my favorite lead sources and are primarily what I built my career on. FSBOs are the easiest of all lead sources to work with, and once you learn the secrets I'm about to tell you, you'll dominate FSBOs in your market!

Homeowners who sell by owner do so for many reasons, but there are two primary reasons you must understand deeply and make peace with. One is they may not understand or place high value on the work that we do as real estate agents, and believe they can do a better job. And two, they want to save money by "not paying commission" (which really means that they want to net as much money as they can).

Now, pay close attention to what I'm about to explain. According to the data, as technology advances, resulting in the real estate transaction becoming more and more complicated, the number of people selling by owner is actually going down, not up as many believe. In fact, the percentage of homes sold by owner in 2019 hit an all-time low of 7%, which is down from the all-time high of 15% in 1981. Why is this happening? There's one major factor that people selling by owner fail to realize at first. In the beginning, when their optimism is at its highest, the FSBO believes that their strategy to sell their home without a Realtor will result in them netting more money in their pocket. In fact, this is not likely to happen. Before I explain why that's the case, promise me you'll never find yourself arguing these next points with a FSBO. It will be a waste of time and you'll lose out on the opportunity.

Make no mistake, it is the goal of a FSBO to sell their home without any agents involved. However, there are two major factors working against them. One is the foundational concept of supply and demand. It's commonly known that when demand is high and supply is low, the higher in value an item becomes. FSBOs fail to take advantage of this market trend because unlike homes listed with a professional real estate company, demand for FSBOs is very low. Thus, they only appeal to a small percentage of the buyer market, and ultimately suffer from a general lack of buyer exposure. Factor two: Think about the FSBO's ideal buyer for a second. This is a buyer who is not represented by an agent, even though buyer representation is free to the buyer! What type of buyer might this be? Ah yes! This is the type of buyer looking for one thing, and one thing only. You guessed it, a deal! This unrepresented buyer knows they can't get away with lowballing houses listed with Realtors because their offers would never be accepted or submitted. So, just like the car buyer looking for a deal on craigslist, these buyers seek out FSBOs and the lowball war begins. If you've been working FSBOs for a while, you'll sometimes have them tell you about dealing with these buyers. This is why I believe in my soul two things about working with FSBOs: One, I can in fact sell their home for more than they can, and two, I can net them more money in their pocket than they can on their own, even after paying commissions.

If you're going to succeed in getting FSBOs to list with you, there are some rules you must follow, some of which are already discussed in Chapter 4. Agents in our coaching program know these as the FSBO Rules of Engagement:

1. **Nothing is as it seems.** Don't take what the FSBO tells you over the phone literally. FSBOs are notorious for telling one agent that they will never list their home and listing with a different agent the very same day.

2. **Never take the bait.** When a FSBO gives you some line about how they don't need an agent or they're not interested in working with an agent, DO NOT ever try to convince them otherwise.

3. **Allow the FSBO to go through the pain of selling their home on their own.** Some FSBOs will sell on their own and some won't. Our best chances of getting FSBO listings are with the ones we have been communicating with and for whom we stand out as the obvious choice when the day comes that they start considering other options—usually four to six weeks in the future. Agents who don't understand this spend their time pissing off FSBOs, trying to convince them to list their home too early in the process. Be patient and play the long game.

4. **Follow-up is the key to converting FSBOs.** Like I mentioned before, the most likely time that a FSBO will decide to list their home is in weeks four through eight. This when their optimism has been beaten out of them by tire-kickers, lowball offers, and knucklehead agents using old outdated high-pressure selling tactics. Your job is to continue to follow up until the day the FSBO sells or until the day they start to look at other options. Your competition is not willing to do this so it will be easy for you to become the obvious choice if you can be patient and follow up consistently over time.

FOR RENT BY OWNERS (FRBOS)

For rent by owners are homeowners who have a rental property for which they are actively seeking out a new tenant. Now, you may find yourself asking, how is this a seller lead? Well, meet my other favorite lead source, the absentee owner. These are homeowners who own another home that, for whatever reason, didn't or could not sell, and they decided to try their hand at being a landlord. Here's a pro tip: The largest percentage of closed transactions are from non-owner-occupied properties, aka, absentee owners. Yes, if you look in your MLS right now and pull a report showing the total number of homes sold, you'll find that there's no single demographic that makes up for more home sales than non-owner occupants. In some markets, I've seen as much as 20% of the total closed transactions coming from this one lead source! It's crazy, right? This is one of the reasons why I like this lead source so much. The other is that competition is extremely low, if there's any at all. It's rare that I find a real estate agent who is actively working FRBOs and other absentee owners. I mean, take yourself as an example. Before reading this book, had you been working this lead source?

So how are FRBOs a seller lead? Well, as I mentioned before, most of these homeowners own one, maybe two, rental properties. They are not full-time investors. For most, these properties are a headache to manage, and in most cases are not producing enough cash flow for it to be worth it. A FRBO is an absentee owner who we know is right in the middle of the worst time for a landlord, which is tenant turnover. This is when these owners deal with the most headache. So if you call them during this time and explain that their property might be worth more than they know, and that they could potentially cash out and end the nightmare of being a landlord, you'll find a large number who would love to take you up on that!

If I haven't yet sold you on calling FRBOs, hopefully this will. I made a video of myself calling FRBOs and other absentee owners on my YouTube channel. You can find it if you just type "Brandon Mulrenin Cold Calling" into the YouTube browser. In less than 30 minutes and on live camera you can watch me generate five listing opportunities. Yes five, and with less than 30 minutes worth of work! Five listings in my market are worth about $35,000 in commissions, which would equal about $70,000 per hour! I don't know about you, but I don't know of any other careers where you can generate $70,000 an hour outside of being a pro athlete, or a famous actor or musician. Does this happen every time I call absentee owners? Not quite. However, it is quite normal for me to generate at least one listing opportunity for every 30 minutes of calling this lead source.

TIPS FOR CALLING FRBOS

Calling FRBOs and absentee owners is probably the easiest kind of prospecting call you'll ever make for reasons already mentioned, and additionally, the script is only one sentence long. When calling FRBOs you want to be enthusiastic about the market and the potential opportunity to cash in, ending the nightmare of being a landlord. Even if you have a prospect tell you they're not considering selling the property, don't give up there; generate a long-term relationship with consistent follow-up instead. There will come a day when they do sell the home, and if you've consistently followed up, you've guaranteed yourself a listing down the road.

PILLAR 2— SPECIALTY NICHES

How many times have you heard this before? Well, in real estate it's true. If you can master a specific market segment or niche that is unique, you'll always have a consistent influx of new clients and new listings. We define a niche as it relates to real estate prospecting as "a specific segment of the market that may have the potential of selling their home, and that is not obvious to our competitors." Here are just some examples that have worked for me as well as for agents I have coached.

Absentee owners, probate, the newly divorced, military veterans, relocation, corporate real estate benefit programs, doctors, teachers, first responders, seniors, free-and-clear properties, likely-to-sells—these are homeowners who have likely lived in the same two-story home for over 20 years, have it paid off, and have significantly more square footage than the average home in your market. And these are often downsizing sellers.

The key is when you choose your niche, you master it. Seriously, go learn every aspect of your niche so that you know more about your niche than anyone in your market. Once you can say this is true, you can then leverage social media content and video content to attract your ideal clients like a magnet. You can interview industry experts in your niche; you can become the known authority in this niche and become known as the go-to agent in your market.

For example, let's pretend you're going to specialize in working with people who are going through a divorce. Why would you pick that niche? It's arguably one of the best niches an agent can specialize in. Think about this. There is one divorce every 36 seconds, nearly 2,400 every day—about 875,000 people get divorced every year. In many of these cases, the divorcing couple sells the marital home for various reasons. In addition, there are many times when each divorcing spouse will buy a new home. That's three potential transactions from one prospect, not to mention the potential mortgage referrals you have for your mortgage partner (more on that shortly). But to really top it off, how many times have you heard about a real estate agent who specializes in divorce real estate? Oh yeah, that's right—never. Do you see now why you'd pick this as a potential niche? But I digress.

Suffice it to say if you did choose this as your niche, you'd want to master it. There are plenty of opportunities to even become certified in divorce real estate! Your goal would be to become the known expert authority on real estate in divorce cases to such a degree that divorce judges would call you into court to testify as an expert witness, and attorneys would pay you to do CMAs. Yes, those are both possible. Imagine a world where you are known as the go-to Realtor when people get divorced and you had every divorce attorney in town referring you to all of their clients to sell their homes. It'd be pretty cool, right? The point is, pick a niche that you're passionate about, that you can master, and where you know competition is scarce.

PILLAR 3—REFERRAL PARTNERS

If you've been a real estate agent for any length of time, you'll understand what I am about to say. According to the National Association of Realtors, there's one job created for every two homes that are sold. So for every 1,000 homes sold, there are 500 additional jobs created. Furthermore, every time a home is sold, there's about $58,000 in revenue that is generated for the local market economy. As a result, real estate agents are one of the biggest prospects for many industries to go after, as they offer massive potential for referral business. Think about it: Does it ever seem to you as though every time your phone rings it's a lender trying to take you to lunch, a title rep trying to meet for coffee, or an insurance agent inviting you to the local sports event? I don't think some agents realize how much value we provide the economy, but when you sit back and think about how many industries exist because of what we do, it's incredible.

Like so many other industries that prospect real estate agents every day in the pursuit of referral business, you, the real estate agent, should be doing the exact same thing. Make a list of industries that, due to the nature of their business, may have clients who are also likely to need the services of a real estate agent who understands their unique situation.

Let me help you get started. Here's a list of referral partners every real estate agent should have as part of their business plan. When you build a relationship with these professionals, you'll start to reap the reward of earning more and more of their referral business.

- Divorce attorneys
- Probate attorneys
- Estate planning attorneys
- Assisted living sales managers
- CPAs
- Financial planners

- Insurance agents
- Caregiving agencies
- Mortgage lenders
- Title insurance reps

All of these professionals deal with clients who have a need to buy and sell real estate. There's a massive opportunity for you to work with these professionals because believe me when I tell you, other agents in your market do not spend time building their referral team. To this day I have two divorce attorneys I've been working with for years who refer two to three listings to me every month from their clients who need to sell as a result of a divorce.

PILLAR 4—SPHERE OF INFLUENCE

This pillar of business is probably the most neglected and most important pillar in a real estate agent's business. The fact is, most agents in the industry got their license just to sell three to four homes a year for friends and family. They don't do anything proactively to work their sphere of influence (SOI); just the mere fact that their friends know they are in real estate results in them selling a few homes here and there.

But for the agent who wants to make a career selling real estate and generate a full-time income where they're able to support their family and accomplish their dreams and goals, their SOI will need to be a big part of their business plan. As a matter of fact, your SOI should begin to make up about 30% to 40% of your business every year if you work the plan I'm going to share with you in this book.

Working directly with people you know (and their referrals) is arguably the best type of business for a few reasons. One, typically people you know will have more respect for your time, as they know more about your personal life and family responsibilities. Two, SOI and referral clients are more enjoyable to work with because of the already existing relationship. This also results in a higher level of personal commitment to the transaction on your end. You are going to make sure these clients will be especially well served. And three, people in your SOI (and their referrals) typically have more appreciation for what you do, your expertise, and the advice you give along the way.

WORKING YOUR SOI DATABASE TO GENERATE REFERRAL BUSINESS

This simple plan, if acted upon, will result in two things occurring that every agent wants, but rarely experiences: 1) to win the top-of-mind awareness game with everyone you know, becoming the go-to person for all things real estate, and 2) to generate a consistent stream of people in your SOI who reach out for your help to buy or sell real estate. This is what you want, right? Then be sure you actually follow this plan and do the work. You don't want to wake up 20 years from now, like so many agents do, still chasing down leads. Your long-term goal as a Realtor should be to build your database every day, follow this plan, and build a referral-based business. And just to be clear, some agents will hear that and say, "Well Brandon, I already have a referral-based business." I'm not talking about becoming an agent who gets three or four referrals a year. I'm talking about a business plan that generates 50, 60, 70-plus closed deals a year that all come from working the Database Plan.

THE DATABASE PLAN OF ACTION

The Database Plan is designed to do exactly what I mentioned just a moment ago—stay top of mind with everyone in your database, and to inspire the people in your database who are looking to buy or sell a home, or people they know looking to buy or sell a home, to call you! The Database Plan has eight strategies that we will cover in detail in this section. The first thing you want to do is organize your database into the following sections.

SECTION 1 – TOP 100

In this section, you're going to include your favorite 100 people. These are people that if you called them to grab lunch or a cup of coffee, it wouldn't be weird. These 100 people would also hire you as their real estate agent without question if they wanted to buy or sell a home. Furthermore, once you execute on all the strategies in the Database Plan, these people will turn into your biggest advocates, referring you to their friends and family at every opportunity. If you don't have 100 people in your life that fit these criteria, start with what you do have and build from there. Maybe you only have 25 people that fit these criteria—that's OK. People in your Top 100 can include, close friends, family, past clients, referral partners, community influencers, and local business owners, just to name a few.

Here's all the information you need for people to be part of your Top 100:

- Connect on Facebook, Instagram and LinkedIn
- Email address
- Birthdate
- Home address
- Cell phone number

Some of the strategies in the Database Plan will only pertain to your Top 100 and others will pertain to everyone in your database.

SECTION 2 – SELLER LEAD DATABASE

In Chapter 9, you'll learn more about how to follow up with your seller leads that you'll be generating daily but here's how you'll want to organize this section of your database inside your CRM. Here's the information you'll want to get to add prospects into your seller lead database.

- Connect on Facebook, Instagram and LinkedIn. Yes you want to add leads that you generate on social media. This is CRITICAL to your conversion ratios. This is how you humanize yourself with prospects.

- Email address

- Home address

- Cell phone number

You'll want to have four categories within this section of your database:

- Leads not contacted

- Hot leads

- Warm leads

- Nurtures

Once you have your database and CRM organized, now you can start executing on each strategy and start generating repeat and referral business.

Strategy 1—Daily Instagram Story

Instagram stories should be used to give the people in your database a behind-the-scenes look into life as a real estate agent. This should help to connect with your database on a level they are not used to seeing you in, when you're in your element working. For example, let's say you're headed out on a listing appointment. You can make a short video telling your followers where you're headed, and a little about the area that makes the potential listing a great place to live. You want to make a story like this five days a week. Yes, Monday through Friday you need a new Instagram story. Both your Top 100 and the people in your seller lead database should see your daily stories.

Strategy 2—Weekly Neighborhood Real Estate Email

Other than being pissed off that you didn't get the listing, what do you think every time you pass a real estate "for sale" sign in your neighborhood? That's' right! "How much is it?" and "I wonder how it compares to my house?" Well, this is the same thing everyone else thinks too. So you have a choice to make. You, the real estate agent in their life, can provide this data to them proactively or they can search Zillow or another competitor's website to get the information. I think everyone reading this book would choose the former. The good news is that every real estate agent has the tool to do just this. You're going to want to set everyone in your database up to receive an automated email from your MLS system that shows the details of the homes for sale, the homes that have accepted offers, and homes that have sold in their neighborhood. You want to ensure everyone in your database receives this email weekly. Both your Top 100 and the people in your seller lead database should receive a weekly neighborhood real estate email.

Strategy 3—Weekly Facebook Live "Show"

Social media can be powerful if you leverage it by providing value to your audience. Too many agents are posting on social media with content no one finds valuable. And in some cases, agents post content that is annoying and that actually turns people off. In addition to your daily Instagram story, you want to plan on posting at least one valuable piece of content weekly. Here's what we teach agents in our coaching program to do.

Don't get intimidated—just hear me out. Imagine if once a week, at the same time, you did a short 10- to 15-minute Facebook Live where you answered some of the most common questions you get from your clients and shared that information with the rest of your audience who may be wondering the same things. There are TONS of topics you could use. Here are just a few examples: Who pays for a home inspection? Can you back out of an offer? What happens if the home does not appraise for the purchase price? Do open houses actually work?

For most people, making videos is something they are not comfortable doing, which is the point! Your competition is not doing it. So you need to get very comfortable being "uncomfortable" if you're going to succeed in this business of real estate sales, trust me. Both your Top 100 and the people in your seller lead database should see your show.

Strategy 4—Monthly Database Letter

Remember our goal with the database plan—to stay top of mind. Here's what's interesting: Historically, if we look to see where the attention of our prospects has been, it's gone from print to digital, and now because of how much digital content there is, print has once again become very effective (not to mention, your competition is not doing it). Each month, you'll want to send a letter to everyone in your database. Unlike social media and email, this strategy ensures that everyone in your database is seeing your face every month. In your monthly letter, you'll want to include the following: A snapshot of the local real estate market numbers over the past month, a short synopsis of what these numbers mean, and something personal about yourself. The key, like anything else, is to be consistent. Only your Top 100 will receive your monthly letter.

Strategy 5—Call Your Top 100 Quarterly

This is the one that most agents have the most trouble with. "But Brandon, what do I say? I don't want to be that annoying agent begging for business." I get it! I don't want you to do that either. Like everything else I teach and believe in, we are going to call with a purpose and provide value. I even give you the exact script to use (in the script section of this book).

Here's what you'll do: In January, you'll call the people in your database to offer an annual "real estate review." Yes, this is another strategy your competition is not doing, and most likely something they've never heard of doing. You'll simply touch base with everyone in your database to:

1. See what their real estate plans are for the year and if they have any desire or thoughts of moving.

2. See if they have any plans to do home renovations.

3. Update them on mortgage rates to see if it might make sense for them to refinance.

4. (The BIG value add), ask about any improvements they've done that might impact the value of their home, as you'll be providing everyone in your database with an annual comparative market analysis of their home's value. This way, the people in your database, those folks you say you care about, always know what their house is worth. Do you think this provides value? Big time! Who do you think they will call if they ever do want to sell? That's right—the agent who knows more about their house than anyone else! You!

In April, you'll call to remind the people in your database to check their AC units and to turn on the water in their sprinkler systems. This might also be a great time to refer them to one of your referrals partners to help them do both. Is it starting to make sense now?

In July, you'll call to invite them to your annual client appreciation event. This can be a simple event that can grow over time. You can start by just doing a barbecue at your home with some bounce houses and a face painter for the kids.

In October, you'll call to remind them to get any furnace maintenance done before winter, and to turn the water off to their sprinkler system. And yes, this is another opportunity for you to provide value by referring someone to do both—or even coordinating it for them!

Strategy 6 – The Birthday Program

Recognizing people on their birthdays has become a lost art and has become noise on social media. This strategy will help to show people how much you do care and continue to earn the top-of-mind awareness. Here's what you'll do. Everyone in your Top 100 should receive a birthday card with a $1 scratch-off lottery ticket in the mail for their birthday each year. In addition, you'll also call each person on their birthday to wish them a happy birthday. This is another great touch throughout the year to continue strengthening your relationship with the folks in your Top 100. If the person does not answer, leave a voicemail wishing them a happy birthday. It's one of the best voicemails to leave and receive.

Strategy 7 – Thanksgiving Letter

Holiday cards have become another thing that we've grown accustomed to sending and receiving without much thought. For many people, the meaning of the card is gone. They receive a pile of holiday cards that stack up just to be thrown away. Think about this: When's the last time you received a Thanksgiving card? And not just a generic Thanksgiving card, a card that was written to you specifically that outlined what you meant to the sender? Well, this is exactly what you'll start sending to your Top 100.

Each year during Thanksgiving, you'll write a card to each person in your Top 100 giving thanks to them for the relationship you have. You'll want to mention specific examples of things you've done together throughout the year with that specific person. For example, let's say you send a Thanksgiving card to one of your divorce attorneys who's a referral partner in your Top 100. You could talk about the golf outing you played in together and how continuing to work together professionally is something you value very much. These letters have been something that has made a HUGE impact with the relationships I have in my Top 100 and it will do the same for you!

Strategy 8 – The Annual Client Event

Hosting events is by far the most impactful thing you can do to pour into relationships. I don't know the exact numbers, but I will tell you this one strategy alone is probably responsible for the majority of my SOI/referral business over the years. You don't need to do anything extravagant in the beginning. Once a year in the summer, you can host a simple barbecue at your home or a local park where you provide food, drinks and a few activities for kids. Pro tip: Get your referral partners to help contribute toward the cost of the annual event each year to help offset the cost. You can then have some promotional items at the event promoting your referral partners in addition to sending them referral business throughout the year. This annual event is something you'll invite your Top 100 to each year and something that will continue to grow over time.

Now be honest, if you actually followed this plan and did this every year, do you think you'd get people in your SOI to hire you as their agent and get them to refer people they know are looking to buy or sell a home? Of course you would! The biggest challenge is actually doing it.

Agents often ask me, "Brandon, how did you sell over 100 homes a year?" The answer, as you now know, is to have four lead generation pillars. Not one, not two, not three, but all four outlined in this book. If you do, you'll never have to worry about where your next deal is coming from again.

8

The Prospecting Plan of Action

To become a great real estate agent and prospector, you'll need to have productivity systems that help you form a new habit of daily prospecting. I treat prospecting and my daily productivity the way an athlete prepares for the big game. If done right, succeeding as an agent who can effectively prospect, generate leads, and set appointments on demand can and will change your life forever. In this chapter, you'll learn the disciplines, routines, and habits of the top real estate salespeople in the world.

YOUR BANK ACCOUNT IS A DIRECT REFLECTION OF YOUR DAILY SCHEDULE

Of all the things real estate agents struggle with, nothing compares to choice-management and managing their time to be as productive as possible. People get into real estate typically coming from the corporate world, where accountability is real—if they didn't show up for work, they got fired. Now, as an independent contractor, they can do whatever they want with their time. But how do they spend it? That's right, they choose the path of least resistance and do anything that will enable them to avoid doing the actual work in this business, which is to pick up the phone and prospect. This is why only the strong will survive in real estate. Most people, left on their own, will fail. They need structure and accountability; otherwise, they simply won't do the work.

At ReverseSelling.com, we coach our agents to break their day up into four quarters—just like a football game, basketball game, or how a business plans its year. Here's a simple framework you can follow that will give your days structure and focus.

First Quarter

This is what we refer to as the morning routine. This is everything you do from the time you wake up until your daily prospecting mission is complete. The first quarter should go from the time you wake up, which should be no later than 6 a.m., and will go to about 10 a.m.

Second Quarter

The second quarter of the day will go from 10 a.m. to 12 noon, or when you break for lunch, and should be spent following up with your leads.

Third Quarter

Unlike the other three quarters, this time of the day should be spent working on your non-revenue generating tasks such as administrative tasks, updating your files, returning calls and email, etc. You can also use this time for additional appointment prep. Your third quarter should go from about 12 to 2 p.m.

Fourth Quarter

This is showtime. The last quarter of the day should be used for listing appointments and face-to-face meetings. This is where it all comes together and what you spend every ounce of your energy trying to get to: The sales appointment, your opportunity to meet with a potential client and, through the value you add at the meeting, obtain a new client.

Note, if you don't have an appointment during this time, there's only ONE thing you need to be doing. Yup, you guessed it—prospecting. Never forget your job: You're either prospecting on the phone generating appointments, or you're on appointments. You should have two appointment slots in your daily schedule, one at 3 p.m. and one at 5 p.m. Your job is to fill those slots and then be home for dinner with your family by 6 p.m.

The Nightly Routine

Plan tomorrow today. This is critical for those who want to be as productive as they can during peak hours of their working day. While the morning routine remains the most important part of the day, which we will talk about here in just a moment, the nightly routine sets you up to succeed in the morning. Here's what we train agents in our coaching program to do each night:

1. Complete any meeting prep for the next day's meetings, including CMAs. You really don't want to spend productive hours doing administration.

2. Be sure you've updated your prospecting tracker so you can start fresh the next day.

3. Reflect on your day. Review your business plan and goals and be honest with what you did well and what you need to be better at the following day.

4. Take a hot shower. Studies have shown that you sleep better after a hot shower. The hot shower helps calm your mind and get you into a relaxed state.

5. Go to sleep at the same time every night. Only now do you hear the world's elite performers talking about the importance of sleep. For years, you had big influencers like Gary V saying that sleep is for the weak. Not anymore. Gary V himself now has new content explaining how important sleep is to your overall performance and productivity. So go to sleep at the same time each night. Be sure the room temperature is a little cooler than where you keep it during the day. Sleep is a secret weapon that no one talks about. Most of your competition

stays up late, going out to dinner, and drinking alcohol until 1 a.m. They end up sleeping in and missing the most productive part of the day—the morning.

The Morning Routine

The morning routine is the holy grail, the one thing that, if executed on consistently, alone has the power to determine your success or failure in this business. Yes, the morning routine is that important. Mastering the morning has two major benefits: 1) is that 80% of your income and results in your business will come from this time block, and will take 20% of your effort, putting the Pareto Principle to work, and 2) the mental toughness you will build. Think about it. You're doing three of the hardest things in life and in business all before 10 a.m., waking up early, working out, and prospecting. Most of the world, and certainly your competition, are weak and the mornings are a struggle. But not you! Master the morning, master your life! Here's what we recommend you do each and every morning without fail and without excuses, even if you don't feel like it.

1. Wake up at the same time every day but no later than 6 a.m.

2. Sweat for 20 to 30 minutes. Exercising will release dopamine and endorphins, which will give you energy, make you feel great, and give you mental clarity and focus. Trust me, you're going to need it.

3. Review your business plan and goals. Visualize yourself doing the work and accomplishing every single one of the goals you've set and think about how that will feel when you do.

4. Take a cold shower. That's right, get your ass in a cold shower every morning. Why? It will build more mental toughness and you will experience health benefits. I can't go deep into this now but do your own research to learn all the reasons why you should take cold showers. Once you get used to it, you'll wonder why you didn't do this before because of how good you will feel!

5. Drink your coffee but skip breakfast. Outdated information suggested that breakfast was the most important meal of the day, but new research, as well as my own experience doing it for two years now, are shedding new light on the tremendous benefits of intermittent fasting. In addition to helping your energy levels stay high and helping you to have incredible mental focus, intermittent fasting can also help you lose weight and burn fat, prevent diabetes, heart conditions, some cancers, and Alzheimer's disease. Intermittent fasting has also been proven to help you live longer. Listen, I'm not a doctor—do your own research, but it's changed my life. I recommend the 16:8 intermittent fasting approach. I skip breakfast and then have a healthy shake at 12 p.m. Then I can eat until 8 p.m. and then nothing again until the next day at 12 p.m. You may be asking yourself, "What on earth does all this have to do with prospecting and succeeding in my sales business?" EVERYTHING! Real estate is a performance-based business, and just like an athlete, singer, dancer, or movie star, we need to have a healthy mind and body if we're going to have the energy and mental toughness needed to be a world-class competitor and be able to deliver on the promises we made to our families.

6. Make your first dial at 8 a.m. sharp! You want to be at your prospecting station ready to make your first call at 8 a.m.! Have you ever heard the saying, "The early bird gets the worm"? Nothing is more true when prospecting. We've talked about the importance of being the first voice, and this will give you that opportunity.

The Prospecting Schedule

Another common question I often get is, "Which lead sources should I call first?" Here's how you should schedule your daily prospecting:

8 a.m. — Dial through all the new expired listings, followed by the fresh FSBOs, and then the fresh FRBOs. This might take you about 45 minutes. I then recommend you go back through the exact same list and dial through all the leads you did not yet contact.

Pro tip: Don't, I repeat, DO NOT be the agent who attempts to call each lead source only once, and then tells me they can't hit their daily contact goal. Studies have shown that it takes on average eight attempts to reach most prospects.

9-9:15 a.m. — You've gone through your new leads and have attempted to contact them more than once. You'll now want to text all of the new leads you didn't contact by phone. Aggressive? YES! How bad do you want it?

10 a.m. — Spend about an hour calling your niche lead pillar and referral partners. These are specific niche lead sources like absentee owners, probates, assisted living, divorce attorneys, etc.

11 a.m. — Focus your attention on lead follow-up. We'll discuss this more in Chapter 9, but this is the time where you'll follow up with leads in your database to ensure no opportunities fall through the cracks.

THE PROSPECTING WATERFALL

It's important not to lose focus on the goal of your prospecting efforts. Make no mistake, your primary objective when making prospecting calls is to set an appointment for a face-to-face meeting, whether it's a listing appointment, preview appointment, or buyer's consultation. Just get in front of that prospect as fast as you can!

If, and only if, you can't get the prospect to agree to the face-to-face meeting, you would go on to the next part of the Prospecting Waterfall, which is to generate a lead. A lead is when you have a good conversation with a prospect, obtain their email address, and both you and the prospect agree to talk again about potentially meeting at some point in the future.

There are many different outcomes that can occur when you successfully generate a lead. It can be a hot lead, where you have an opportunity to meet with the prospect in a few days, or it can be a warm lead, or what we call a seller nurture, whom you'll want to follow up with weekly because they have expressed a desire to buy or sell six to 12 months or more into the future.

Finally, the only other outcome that can occur on a prospecting call is when the call goes nowhere, or the prospect is completely unreasonable or rude. These prospects need to be deleted from your prospecting database.

So to be clear, here are the possible outcomes of the Prospecting Waterfall and what to focus on:

1. You set the appointment.

2. You try to set an appointment but are unsuccessful, so you generate a hot lead.

3. You generate a warm lead.

4. You generate a seller nurture.

5. You delete the lead from your prospecting database.

PROSPECTING RATIOS AND TRACKING YOUR NUMBERS

There's no doubt that having clear goals is something no one will argue with. I will make the argument, however, that it's just as important to have a plan that outlines how you'll go about accomplishing those goals. Goal-setting has become popular among the real estate agent community. What I find disturbing is when I ask to see the plan that outlines what needs to be done to accomplish the goals, it's rare that anything can be found. In this section, I'll specify average prospecting conversion ratios that will clearly lay out what needs to be done to achieve your goals. Remember, these are averages and your ratios will be different, which is why it's critical that you track your numbers. What gets measured and tracked gets improved. It's that simple.

Professional athletes, Fortune 500 companies, and small businesses track their numbers. For some reason, real estate agents are the only people who call themselves business owners who don't track their numbers. It's weird, I know. So be sure you track each conversion ratio that we will discuss in this section. Once you start to establish your own averages, you'll know with absolute certainty how many dials it takes to have a conversation, how many conversations it takes you to set an appointment, and how many appointments it takes to get a listing. There's great power in this. When you know your numbers intimately, you'll be inspired to take action as you'll now know exactly what you need to do to make any amount of income that you desire. You can download the prospecting tracker that the agents in our coaching program use at ReverseSelling.com.

AVERAGE PROSPECTING CONVERSION RATIOS

Let's say your goal is to earn $100,000 per year by listing and selling homes, which seems to be most agents' number. First, we need to look at the average commission earned per transaction. Every agent is on a different commission split, so let's use an average commission of $5,000 per home sold. This is before tax, but after your brokerage split. This means you would have to sell 20 homes to reach your income goal of $100,000.

Second, we need to look at how many listings you must take to sell 20 homes, because not every listing you take will sell. On average, and in this market, we are seeing about 70% of the listings an agent takes actually sell. This can be because the seller decides not to sell, the listing was overpriced, or a host of other reasons why agents sometimes fail to get the home sold. Using a 70% list-to-sold ratio, we see that to sell 20 homes, you must take about 30 listings.

Third, to get 30 listings you'll need to go on 60 listing appointments, as we've learned the average close ratio is about 50%.

Fourth, to go on 60 listing appointments you'll need to schedule about 75 of them because 20% of your appointments won't happen, due to cancellations on either end. Either way, you should build your business plan with an 80% listing appointment kept ratio.

Next, what do you need to do to set 75 appointments? The vast majority of your listing appointments will come from prospects you've met with in person, or from leads you've been following up with. On average, it takes about 50 real conversations with prospects, through face-to-face preview appointments or through your weekly lead follow-up efforts, to set one listing appointment. This means that to set 75 listing appointments in one year you'll need to have about 3,750 prospecting conversations over the course of the year, which breaks down to about 15 to 20 per day.

And finally, to have 15 to 20 prospecting conversations per day, you'll need to prospect for at least two hours every day, five days a week, for the entire year. On average, if you're on a dialer, and getting quality leads from a prospecting platform (which we will discuss next), you should be able to have about eight to 10 conversions per hour.

To sum up, and to ensure you have a crystal-clear understanding of what you need to do, if you want to achieve your income goal, here's an example of what your simple 12-month listing-based business plan could look like (working backward from your goal):

- Earn $100,000 gross income.
- Take 30 listings.
- Go on 60 listing appointments.
- Set 75 listing appointments.
- Talk with 3,750 prospects over the year.
- Prospect for at least two hours each day, at a minimum.
- Talk with 15 to 20 prospects per day.

It doesn't get any clearer than that.

RECOMMENDED PROSPECTING PLATFORMS

There are many companies that provide phone numbers for expired listings, FSBOs, FRBOs, and other lead sources, all of which have their advantages and disadvantages. The important thing is that you get one immediately. You cannot afford to waste your time searching the internet for hours each day, looking for phone numbers, and trying to keep your leads organized. In my experience using different platforms for over 15 years, I believe that Vulcan 7 currently has the best platform. They have the best lead quality, the technology is easy to use, and the system makes it simple to keep your leads organized. You can get a discount to use the Vulcan 7 platform by going to www.Vulcan7.com/brandonmulrenin.

YOUR PROSPECTING STATION

You should have a workspace that is dedicated as your prospecting station, somewhere that you can be focused with minimal distractions. This is your Zen place—the place where you do your best work. Make it comfortable; have your vision board displayed, and hang pictures on the walls that inspire greatness! Your prospecting station should be clean and organized. Ideally, it should offer the option to stand while making prospecting calls to keep your energy level high. It needs to be a place you look forward to going to every day.

9

The Fortune is Made in the Follow-Up

THE FORTUNE IS MADE IN THE FOLLOW-UP

This saying, although very popular, is absolutely true, and something you need to fully understand if you're ever going to reach your full potential in real estate sales. To illustrate this, I now call your attention to something I call pipeline maturity. Here's how it works. Rarely will you set an actual listing appointment on the first conversation with a prospect—maybe only about 5 to 10% of the time. Instead, about 90% of your listing appointments (and therefore your listings) will come from following up with prospects. It sometimes takes six, eight, 10 or more times, or sometimes longer, but if you stay in touch, you'll reap the reward.

Pro tip: When I was selling 100 homes a year, more than 50% of my business (and we're talking over $500,000 in personal income) came from a prospect who I followed up with for more than six months!

Here's some more of the worst advice ever given to real estate agents by some of the famous gurus: "If the lead is not ready to sign a contract in seven to 10 days, throw away the lead." This is total crap! Only someone who doesn't actually sell real estate would give this advice, because in reality, about nine out of 10 times, it takes longer than seven to 10 days of following up with and nurturing a prospect before they are ready to sign a listing contract or submit an offer on a home. This is why I have so much frustration that the "gurus," the ones giving sales advice to real estate agents, don't even sell real estate themselves—and in some cases, they have NEVER sold real estate. But I digress. The point is, some prospects will take a week to convert into a new client, and some will take a year. In either case, you will need to have a lead follow-up system that allows you to benefit from leads in your pipeline that will mature and eventually manifest into business.

This is the area many agents struggle with the most, and for many reasons—addiction to instant gratification and a lack of systems, to name just a couple. If you really understand the concept of pipeline maturity, you will recognize that 80 to 90% of your business will come from following up with prospects over time. If you fail to accept this, or more importantly, take it seriously, and do something about it, you'll be losing out on 80 to 90% of the business you could be getting.

PROSPECTING SELLER LEAD DATABASE ORGANIZATION

If you have not done so already, go and get yourself a prospecting platform/lead provider, like Vulcan 7. Once you have done this, and you have your prospecting platform up and running, here's how you'll arrange the folders inside the system to ensure that you stay organized, and make sure no lead falls through the cracks.

Folder 1—Leads Not Contacted

Your lead provider will automatically upload the new Expired Listings, FSBOs, and FRBOs to your system every day. You'll want to have a folder where you put leads you have tried to call but have not yet made contact with. This folder represents an area most agents struggle with when prospecting—we call it the black hole. Agents are great at calling fresh leads once, but terrible at making multiple attempts. And when you ask them why, they usually come up with nothing. Studies have shown it takes on average eight attempts before making contact with a prospect. This may be the reason so many agents fail to hit their prospecting goals: They're only attempting to contact new leads once or twice!

THE BLACK HOLE PREVENTION PLAN

Immediately after you've attempted to contact a lead without success, before moving on to the next dial, place the lead into the "Leads No Contact" folder inside your prospecting database. Then you'll want to attempt to contact these leads multiple times on day one and subsequently each day until you make contact. In time, this will be your largest folder of leads, requiring more time spent in lead follow-up.

Folder 2—Hot Leads

We define a "hot lead" as a prospect you have spoken to who has agreed to receive a follow-up call at an agreed-upon time in the future, has provided you with their contact information, including email address, and is actively looking to hire a real estate agent. This is a prospect you have the opportunity to meet with in the next few days to try and earn their business. You'll create another folder in your system labeled "Hot Leads" where you'll put any lead fitting these criteria.

Hot Lead Follow-Up Plan

At a minimum, you should look at hot leads daily to determine if contact is needed. There can never be a day where you don't review the leads in your Hot Lead folder. In most cases, you'll actually want to make contact with prospects in this folder daily, as it is your goal to aggressively follow up. Follow-up is a part of the interview process. You want the prospect to experience how on top of things you are, and you want them to know that you can be counted on. "But Brandon, isn't this a little too much?" No! I've never lost a listing because the prospect said I followed up too much. However, there have been countless times when I have lost listings due to lack of follow-up.

Pro tip: I literally carry around my five hottest leads, either on a lead sheet or 3x5 index card, and every night, before I go home at the end of the day, I call all five of these prospects. I can't tell you how effective this strategy has been for me over the years. Think about it. Most of your contacts will most likely be made in the early morning hours, and your prospects are not used to agents calling in the evening; this allows you to get more of them on the phone. They are also typically in a very different frame of mind in the evening than they were in the morning and are actually impressed when you call later in the day to follow up. As a result of this strategy alone, I probably set more listing appointments in these 15 minutes of the day than in all of the other hours spent prospecting that day combined.

Folder 3—Warm Leads

"Warm Leads" as we define them in this book are prospects who have expressed an interest in meeting with us, but not for a couple of weeks, or even a few months out. This folder is usually made up of mostly FSBOs and Expired Listing leads. Outside of your "Leads Not Contacted" folder, this will be your second most popular folder of leads. This folder is also where you'll spend the most time, energy, and effort as the opportunities presented in this folder are the most lucrative in your entire pipeline.

Warm Lead Follow-Up Plan

Warm leads require an aggressive follow-up plan because these prospects are typically being hunted by multiple agents at the same time. Typically, the last agent standing is the one who wins the listing. The goal of this follow-up plan is to stay top of mind and be there at the very moment the prospect is ready to start interviewing agents.

First, you'll want to schedule time every Monday to call every lead in this folder. You'll call to check in, to see if their plans have changed, or reference the weekly email you'll be sending. Then, when the time is right, ask for what you want—a listing appointment.

Next, every prospect in this folder should receive an email from you every week. To make it as simple as possible, and give actual value to prospective clients, you'll set every warm lead up in your MLS system to receive a weekly email containing the Active, Pending, and Sold listings in and around their neighborhood. This is the information they want, trust me. Instead of the prospect having to search on Zillow or a competitor's website to see what's going on in their neighborhood in terms of home values, they will be looking at your email with your face and contact information every week! This also gives you something tangible to reference when you make your weekly follow-up calls.

In addition to weekly calls, and a weekly email, you also want to communicate with the prospect through their mailbox. That's right! Direct mail is once again very effective because your competition is not doing it, and people are often overwhelmed with the amount of digital content they consume. We recommend you use a company called Mailbox Power. This company allows you to set up an automated drip campaign, just like we do with emails. This way, your prospects will get a weekly mailer from you automatically after you set them up in the system one time! Go to www.mailboxpower.com/reverseselling to learn more.

Finally, to complete the "Warm Lead Follow-Up Plan," you'll want to text each prospect in this folder every Friday. This text works great because the prospect is likely to think about you over the weekend, which transitions perfectly into your Monday follow-up call. This is a simple text that will say, "Mr. Prospect, it's Brandon with Brookstone Realtors. I'll be available all weekend if you need anything. Do you need help with anything right now?" This is another touch that is helping you to pour into the relationship as you continue to communicate from a place of contribution.

To recap, warm leads, like FSBOs, Expired Listings, and sometimes FRBOs, require an aggressive follow-up strategy as you have the highest likelihood of setting a listing appointment and earning new business from this group.

Folder 4—Seller Nurtures

The last category and folder you'll need to set up in your prospecting database is a folder for "Seller Nurtures." These are prospects that have a need to buy, or sell, but not until some specified future point in time, typically six to 12 months or more. For this folder add prospects with whom you have a good conversation, those who have agreed to speak with you again and have given you their contact information, including their email address. Don't force leads into your pipeline.

There's nothing more deflating than having leads in your pipeline that are not actual leads.

The Seller Nurture Follow-Up Plan

Prospects in your long-term Seller Nurture folder should also receive the weekly MLS email including Active, Pending, and Sold listing data. In addition, before you end the call with the prospect, you'll want to ask the prospect when they think they might want to buy or sell, and schedule a follow-up call in half that amount of time. At that point, once you've called the prospect and have confirmed that they are still on track for their timelines to buy or sell, you'll want to call once a month leading up to that timeframe. Many times something will happen and their timelines will change. You don't want to miss the opportunity because you waited too long to call. Seller nurtures should also receive the same monthly letter that your SOI database is receiving. Again, your goal is to stay top of mind and be the obvious choice when the time comes for the prospect to hire an agent.

10 | Reverse Selling Scripts

As technology continues to advance, marketers will continue to come out with new gadgets and distractions, promising you can succeed in real estate without prospecting and without having to deal with any rejection. It's my goal that although these offers seem extremely enticing at first, you now know the truth. You must proactively reach out to people you know, and people you don't know, to achieve the goals that you've set.

It's also my goal that this book has helped to change your mindset around what it means to be a salesperson—that proactively reaching out to people no longer brings you pain but becomes something that brings you joy and something you are proud of when you do it. Why? Because you're an expert and the people in your community need your help and deserve to work with an expert like you—someone who cares, who is a master of the market, and who knows how to communicate in a way that helps the client achieve their real estate goals.

You now possess the mindset and skills and have learned exactly what to do to achieve the goals you've set. These three pillars are all you need to succeed. The only question left unanswered is, will you execute? Will you face the truth, fight off your inner demons, and pay the price so you can live the life you desire? A life that you dreamed of when you first got into real estate and a life you promised your family?

If you do the work outlined in this book, there's no doubt you will not only be at the top of all the leaderboards in your market, you will in fact be part of a small, but life-changing group of people that make up the top 20% of the real estate industry. It's my hope that one day I'll see you at the top!

Listing Agent Playbook

Circle Prospecting Script

Sphere of Influence/Past Client Script

FSBO 1.0 Script

FSBO 2.0 Script

Expired Listing Script 1.0

Expired Listing Script 2.0

FRBO Script

Absentee Owner Script

Probate Script

Referral Partner Script

Home Value Script

ZBuyer Script

Price Adjustment Script

Follow Up Scripts

Upfront Listing Agreement Script

Responding To Objections

Reverse Selling Appointment Setting Scripts

Reverse Selling Listing Consultation Script

CIRCLE PROSPECTING SCRIPT

1. Hi, *(Name)*?

2. This is Brandon, I'm a local Realtor and I'm not sure now's the right time, but I was hoping to tell you why I was calling and then you can decide if we should continue or not, fair enough?

3. Great! I'm calling because there are buyers looking for a home just like yours in your neighborhood willing to pay a premium and I was curious if you had plans on moving in the future?

4. OK great! I absolutely love your neighborhood, what has you thinking about moving?

5. Got it, and where are you planning to move once this home sells?

6. Makes sense, and ideally, when would you like to make the move?

7. All of that sounds exciting, well let's do this and really, I don't mind, I'll email you a copy of my resume for you to review and when the time comes, I'd love to see your home and share what I do to get homes like yours sold, would that be fair?

8. OK what's the best email for you typically?

9. I'll send you an email and I'll follow up in *(timeframe discussed,)* fair enough?

SPHERE OF INFLUENCE/PAST CLIENT SCRIPT

January Call - Annual Real Estate Review

1. Hi, *(Name)*?

2. Hi *(Name)*, it's Brandon Mulrenin, how are you?

3. That's good to hear, I'm calling because as you know, in the beginning of the year I like to touch base to see what your real estate plans are for the year?

4. OK got it and are you planning to do any home renovations?

5. OK great and with mortgage rates being around *(X)*, do you think it might make sense to consider refinancing?

6. Makes sense, well like I do every year, I'll be emailing you a detailed pricing analysis on your home for your records, any big changes to the house that could impact the value?

7. OK great, well it was great catching up, is there anything else I can help with at this time?

8. Yes, no worries, and please, if you hear of anyone out there looking to buy or sell their home, would you call me to let me know?

9. Thank you for that! Well look out for the pricing analysis and let me know if you have any questions, talk soon!

April Call - AC/Water

1. Hi, *(Name))*?

2. Hi *(Name)*, it's Brandon Mulrenin, how are you?

3. That's good to hear, I'm calling because as you know, in the beginning of spring, I like to remind everyone to get their water turned back on, get their sprinklers going and get their AC unit checked out, do you need any help with those items this year?

4. OK great, well it was great catching up, is there anything else I can help with at this time?

5. Yes, no worries, and please, if you hear of anyone out there looking to buy or sell their home, would you call me to let me know?

6. Thank you for that! Well, look out for the pricing analysis and let me know if you have any questions, talk soon!

July Call - Annual Client Event

1. Hi, *(Name)*?

2. Hi *(Name)*, it's Brandon Mulrenin, how are you?

3. That's good to hear, I'm calling to invite you and the family to my annual client appreciation event on (date), do you know if you're around?

4. OK great, it should be a good time, we're going to have...

5. I'm also going to send you a reminder in the mail and I'll look forward to seeing you guys soon!

October Call - Furnace/Water

1. Hi, *(Name)*?

2. Hi *(Name)*, it's Brandon Mulrenin, how are you?

3. That's good to hear, I'm calling because as you know, in the beginning of fall, I like to remind everyone to get their water turned off, sprinklers blown out and get their furnace checked, do you need any help with those items this year?

4. OK great, well it was great catching up, is there anything else I can help with at this time?

5. Yes, no worries, and please, if you hear of anyone out there looking to buy or sell their home, would you call me to let me know?

6. Thank you for that! Well, look out for the pricing analysis and let me know if you have any questions, talk soon!

FSBO 1.0 SCRIPT

TIP: This script is designed to get you a high quantity of FSBO preview appointments. You want to use this script and approach for your first 30 to 60 days going after FSBOs or until you've gone on about 20 to 30 FSBO preview appointments. Once you've mastered this, you can move to FSBO script 2.0.

1. Hi *(Name)*?

2. This is Brandon, I'm a local Realtor and I'm not sure now's the right time, but I was hoping to tell you why I was calling and then you can decide if we should continue or not, fair enough?

3. OK great! I'm calling about that home for sale on Main Street and I understand you're selling for sale by owner, is that right?

4. Got it, I absolutely respect that and think it's smart in this market regardless of what other Realtors may say, I was curious if you're open to the idea of a Realtor bringing you a potential buyer for the home?

5. Perfect! I was planning to preview some homes like yours this week before getting to work and was hoping to see yours as well, will you be home tomorrow afternoon between 4 and 6 p.m. to show me the home if I was able to stop by quickly?

6. Great! I'll plan on seeing the home tomorrow right around 4 p.m. and in the meantime, I'll email you my agent information so you have that on file, what's the best email for you typically?

7. Got it, I'm looking forward to seeing your home tomorrow, have a great day!

FSBO 2.0 SCRIPT

TIP: This script is designed to identify potential listing opportunities and increase the quality of your FSBO appointments. This script should be used to set quality listing appointments with FSBOs.

1. Hi *(Name)*?

2. This is Brandon, I'm a local Realtor and I'm not sure now's the right time, but I was hoping to tell you why I was calling and then you can decide if we should continue or not, fair enough?

3. OK, great! I'm calling about that home for sale on Main Street and I understand you're selling for sale by owner, is that right?

4. Got it, I absolutely respect that regardless of what other Realtors may say, I was curious, if you're unable to get the property sold on your own in the next few weeks, would you consider meeting with me to potentially look at some other options?

5. Perfect! I love your neighborhood and the home looks great from what I see online, what has you thinking about moving?

6. I see and in a perfect world, how soon would you like to move?

7. What I'd like to do, is simply stop by one day this week to look at the home and when I'm there, I can walk you through how my FSBO backup plan works and then you can decide if it's something you'd consider doing at this time or not, because obviously you're not going to do anything unless it made sense, right?

8. I can potentially meet you on Tuesday or Wednesday afternoon between 4 and 6 p.m., which works better for you?

9. Perfect, I'll put you in my calendar and I'll send you an email with a copy of my resume so you can review how my plan works, what's the best email to use?

10. Before I let you go, I just have a few quick questions so I can prepare for our meeting…*(Use Upfront Listing Agreement Script)*

EXPIRED LISTING SCRIPT 1.0

TIP: When calling expired listings, be genuinely curious. With script 1.0, your focus should be on getting the face-to-face appointment.

1. Hi *(Name)*?

2. This is Brandon, I'm a local Realtor and I'm not sure now's the right time, but I was hoping to tell you why I was calling and then you can decide if we should continue or not, fair enough?

3. Great! I'm calling about the home for sale on Main Street that came off the market, did you end up accepting an offer?

4. I was curious, are you still considering offers on the property if it made sense?

5. OK great, I was hoping to stop by one day this week to preview the home before getting to work, are you able to show me the home quickly tomorrow afternoon or would Thursday evening be better?

6. OK great, well I'll email you a copy of my information as soon as we hang up for your records, what's the best email for you typically?

7. I'll plan on stopping by around 4 p.m. tomorrow and if anything changes, I'll let you know.

EXPIRED LISTING SCRIPT 2.0

TIP: When calling expired listings, be genuinely curious. Don't give in or give up on the initial resistance; push through to the next question on the script.

1. Hi *(Name)*?

2. This is Brandon, I'm a local Realtor and I'm not sure now's the right time, but I was hoping to tell you why I was calling and then you can decide if we should continue or not, fair enough?

3. OK great! I'm calling about the home for sale on Main Street that came off the market, did you end up accepting an offer or is the home still available by chance?

4. I was curious, are you still considering offers on the property if the offer made sense?

5. I was a little surprised that the home didn't sell, what kind of feedback did your last agent give you?

6. Aww...I see, what do you think stopped the home from selling?

7. Got it, I was calling because I specialize in selling homes that other agents failed to sell and was curious, if you'd be open to meeting with me so that I can share with you maybe why the home didn't sell and then potentially share a plan with you that will cause your home to actually sell if that what you choose because you're not going to do anything unless it made sense, right?

8. I can potentially meet you on Tuesday or Wednesday afternoon between 4 and 6 p.m., which works better for you?

9. Perfect, I'll put you in my calendar and I'll send you an email with a copy of my resume so you can review how my plan works, what's the best email to use?

10. Before I let you go, I just have a few quick questions so I can prepare for our meeting... *(Use Upfront Listing Agreement Script)*

FRBO SCRIPT

1. Hi *(Name)*?

2. This is Brandon, I'm a local Realtor and I'm not sure now's the right time, but I was hoping to tell you why I was calling and then you can decide if we should continue or not, fair enough?

3. OK great! I'm calling about the home for rent on Main Street and was curious with the market so high right now if you'd consider selling the home if the numbers made sense?

4. Great, well what I'd like to do and I really don't mind is do a price analysis on the property, email you the results and if the numbers make sense, we can talk about possibly getting together to discuss a plan to get the property sold, sound fair?

5. Perfect, what's the best email for you typically?

6. Great, I just have a few questions about the property so I can be as accurate as possible with the analysis without seeing the home:

    a. Any major updates that would impact the value of the property?

    b. Finished basement?

    c. Garage?

7. Let me get to work on the analysis and I'll circle back with you this afternoon or this evening, fair enough?

ABSENTEE OWNER SCRIPT

1. Hi *(Name)*?

2. This is Brandon, I'm a local Realtor and I'm not sure now's the right time, but I was hoping to tell you why I was calling and then you can decide if we should continue or not, fair enough?

3. Great! I'm calling about the home on Main Street, are you still the owner?

4. OK great! I was curious if you would consider selling that property while the market is so high?

5. Great, well what I'd like to do and I really don't mind, is do a price analysis on the property, email you the results and if the numbers make sense, we can talk about possibly getting together to discuss a plan to get the property sold, sound fair?

6. Perfect, what's the best email for you typically?

7. Great, I just have a few questions about the property so I can be as accurate as possible with the analysis without seeing the home:

    a. Any major updates that would impact the value of the property?

    b. Finished basement?

    c. Garage?

8. Let me get to work on the analysis and I'll circle back with you this afternoon or this evening, fair enough?

PROBATE SCRIPT

1. Hi *(Name)*?

2. This is Brandon, I'm a local Realtor and I'm not sure now's the right time, but I was hoping to tell you why I was calling and then you can decide if we should continue or not, fair enough?

3. OK great! I'm calling about the property on Main Street and I understand that you might be the person handling the estate at this time, is this correct?

4. Now *(Name)*, I understand how overwhelming the process can be and that's why I'm calling,

5. I specialize in working with people that have real estate going through the probate process *(Name)*, and I was curious, are you planning to keep the property or do you possibly need help preparing the property in the future to be sold?

6. Makes sense, now *(Name)*, I work with a team that can help you get the property cleaned out, make any small repairs and handle an estate sale if needed, I'm wondering if it makes sense for us to possibly schedule a time to meet at the property one day to assess what needs to be done, I'm available tomorrow afternoon or Thursday, would one of those days work for you?

REFERRAL PARTNER SCRIPT

TIP: Every real estate agent should have the following referral partners in their business. 3-4 divorce attorneys, 3-4 financial planners, 3-4 probate/estate attorneys, 3-4 CPAs, 3-4 mortgage loan officers, 3-4 property and casualty insurance agents.

1. Hi *(Name)*?

2. This is Brandon, I'm a local Realtor and I'm not sure now's the right time, but I was hoping to tell you why I was calling and then you can decide if we should continue or not, fair enough?

3. OK great! I'm calling because I understand you specialize in *X*, is that correct?

4. OK perfect! Believe it or not my real estate practice also specializes in *X* and based on what I see online it seems like you focus mainly in the *X* area, is that correct?

5. OK great! Now *(Name)*, I'm looking to work with a top *X* in *X* where we can potentially refer business to each other and I was curious if you have a true real estate professional that specializes in *X* that you work with?

6. No! OK well if you thought it made sense, I'd be happy to grab breakfast or lunch with you one day this week, are you free tomorrow or maybe Friday?

HOME VALUE SCRIPT

1. Hi *(Name)*?

2. This is Brandon, I'm a local Realtor and I'm not sure now's the right time, but I was hoping to tell you why I was calling and then you can decide if we should continue or not, fair enough?

3. Great! I'm calling because I just received notification that you're looking for an accurate home value analysis, is that right?

4. OK great! Now *(Name)*, I just had a few questions about the property and then I can email you a detailed analysis, now are you considering selling the home at some point if it made sense?

5. Got it. So I'll firm up some details about the home really quick and then I'll email you the analysis, if the numbers make sense, you and I can talk about possibly getting together to review a plan to get the home on the market and getting it sold, sound fair?

6. Perfect, now tell me, what major improvements have you made to the home that would impact the value...?

ZBUYER SCRIPT

1. Hi *(Name)*?

2. This is Brandon, I'm a local Realtor and I'm not sure now's the right time but I was hoping to tell you why I was calling and then you can decide if we should continue or not, fair enough?

3. Great! I'm calling because I received notification that you're considering selling the home on Main Street if it made sense, is that correct?

4. OK great! Now *(Name)*, I'm just curious, what has you thinking about selling this property?

5. I see, and if everything works out the way you plan, when would you ideally like to move?

6. Got it, well if you want and really, I don't mind, I can stop by one day, take a look at the property and when I'm there, I can share a plan with you that will cause the home to sell for top dollar and we can talk about if working together might make sense or not, does that sound fair?

PRICE ADJUSTMENT SCRIPT

1. Hi *(Name)*, this is Brandon, is now still a good time?

2. Great, so I sent you an email with a few reports that I'd like to review with you, are you able to review those with me now?

3. Perfect, so the biggest concern I have is the length of time we've been on the market in comparison to the other homes that are selling on average of 17 days, like we've discussed, do you see that on the report?

4. OK so you can see that the other homes that we're competing with have been on the market for less time than we have and have already accepted an offer which means,

5. Our home is helping the other homes to sell vs. the other way around,

6. So, we have to make a decision to either adjust the price to stay in line with the market or risk becoming a stale listing if we stay on the market too long, so I'm

7. Going to recommend we adjust the price to *X*, immediately, what are your thoughts?

FOLLOW-UP SCRIPTS

FSBO

TIP: The purpose of the follow up call is to 1) set a listing appointment and 2) stay top of mind. You must be transparent and ask for what you want and listen closely for the opportunity to set the listing appointment.

1. Hi *(Name)*, it's Brandon from Brookstone Realtors and I'm calling to see if you accepted an offer over the weekend or if the home is still available by chance?

2. I sent you an email last week that shows what's going on with the other homes you're competing with, did you see that home on 123 Main Street (go up for sale, accept an offer, sell?)

3. Did you have a chance to review my FSBO backup plan that I emailed you last week?

4. Great, and I'm wondering if we should meet this week to discuss my plan to get the home sold assuming I can get you the money you need, would you be open to meeting one day this week?

Hot Lead

1. Hi *(Name)*, it's Brandon with Brookstone Realtors and I'm calling to see if we can schedule a good time to meet, I'm actually going to be in your neighborhood tomorrow, can you meet at 4 or 6 p.m.?

Nurture

1. Hi *(Name)*, it's Brandon with Brookstone Realtors and I was calling because, when we spoke last, you were thinking about selling your home in X, is that still the case?

2. Great! I'd like to schedule some time to come see the home and review a plan that will cause your home to sell for a premium, are you around today at 6 p.m. or would tomorrow work better?

UPFRONT LISTING AGREEMENT SCRIPT

1. I have a few questions to ask so that I'm prepared for our meeting so that you get the most from our time together, is that fair?

2. When the home sells, where are you planning to move?

3. Got it, and how soon would you like that to happen?

4. Will you need time after we close to live in the home as you're making the move?

5. Got it, now, is it an option to stay in the home, maybe rent it or have you decided that you'd like to sell at this point?

6. What improvements have you made to the home since living there that might impact the home's selling price?

7. I'm going to send you an email with a detailed pricing analysis that will allow you to look at comparable homes and my listing plan of action, can you review that prior to our meeting?

8. Our meeting should be about 30 minutes and we'll cover a pricing strategy that will cause your home to sell for a premium, we'll review all the numbers and then at the end of our meeting, we can discuss if working together makes sense, does that sound fair?

9. Perfect, now how much should I use for the mortgage payoff as I'm working up the numbers, roughly?

10. Got it, and do you have any questions at this time or is there anything you want to be sure we cover when we meet?

11. Great, I'll look forward to our meeting on *X & X*.

RESPONDING TO OBJECTIONS

5 STEPS TO RESPOND TO ANY OBJECTION

1 – Agreeable Acknowledgement

2 – Strategic Empathy

3 – Assumptive Statement

4 – Value Statement

5 – Gain Agreement

"I'M NO LONGER INTERESTED IN SELLING"

1. Makes sense,

2. and If I was you, I'd feel the same way, so let me ask you,

3. If you got a great offer, it made sense and it helped you move to XYZ, is this something you would at least consider?

4. So let's do this, let's not agree to anything over the phone, what I'd like to do is stop by the home one day this week, share new information that will cause your home to sell and from there, you can decide if working with me might be an option down the road, does that sound reasonable?

"DO YOU HAVE A BUYER?"

1. Great question,

2. And I'm sure you're getting a ton of calls from agents,

3. I don't want to mislead you and tell you I have a buyer right now when I don't, I'm previewing some homes that just went up for sale just like yours and was hoping to see yours too, are you around tomorrow between 4 and 6 p.m. to show me the home quickly?

"I WANT TO WAIT TO SELL"

1. That makes sense,

2. And I can see why you would wait until…, so let me ask you,

3. Obviously you're not going to do anything unless it made sense but, If I showed you a plan that caused your home to sell for a premium right now and allowed you to move to X, would you consider meeting with me one day this week?

"I HAVE A FRIEND IN THE BUSINESS"

1. Certainly, and

2. It's rare to talk to someone these days that doesn't know a Realtor,

3. Which is why it might still make sense for us to meet, because

4. Obviously, you're not going to do anything unless it made sense, but what I've found is that people value more than one option to get perspective and chances are that you do business with your friend, but,

5. If the day ever came where you decided to hire an agent, maybe we can still meet so you can see what other top agents are doing to sell homes like yours and you could at least explore all your options, does that sound reasonable?

"I'M NOT INTERESTED IN WORKING WITH AN AGENT"

1. I totally understand, and

2. In this market, you'll probably have no issue selling the home on your own, which is why I'm calling,

3. If in 30 days from now, by some off chance you're not able to sell on your own, would you at least consider meeting with me to review other options?

"I'M GOING TO USE THE SAME AGENT"

1. *(Name)*, that makes sense and,

2. Using the same agent certainly is the easy choice which is why it might still make sense for us to meet because let's face it,

3. You're not going to do anything unless it makes sense, and so if we met to review a new plan and a different strategy to get your home actually sold that maybe your current agent is not doing, having all your options on the table before making any decisions would make sense, would you agree?

"HOW MUCH DO YOU CHARGE?"

1. Great question and the money you net after the sale is critically important which is why,

2. I offer my flexible commission program which will be one if the first things we discuss when we meet to ensure you net the most money bottom line which is obviously our goal,

3. Right?

"WE'RE GOING TO KEEP THE PROPERTY AS A RENTAL"

1. Makes sense with the rental market being so hot, and so,

2. If property values keep going up, would you consider selling the property in the future to cash out if you end up not wanting to be a landlord?

"WILL YOU CUT YOUR COMMISSION?"

V1

1. Great question,

2. And obviously if I'm you, I would look to ensure I net the most money, bottom line,

3. which is what you want, regardless of the commission right?

4. Makes total sense,

5. And I'm sure there are many agents that would drop their commission in a second to get your listing which would absolutely be a red flag, can I share why?

6. If an agent is that quick to lower their OWN income, which they use to feed their family, how fast do you think they would want you to lower your price or worse yet, negotiate a lower offer price with another agent just to get the deal done?

7. So, let's do this, I feel 100% confident that I can get your home sold and if you're comfortable with me, let's go ahead and move forward and if there's ever a day that you feel different, you have the right to fire me at anytime, is that reasonable?

V2

1. Great question,

2. And obviously if I'm you, I would look to ensure I net the most money, bottom line,

3. which is what you want, regardless of the commission right?

4. Makes total sense,

5. And I'm sure there are many agents that would drop their commission in a second to get your listing, which would absolutely be a red flag, can I share why?

6. So if we look at the real estate commission structure, it's important to understand how it works...If we take a 3% commission, I think the assumption sometimes is that the entire 3% goes to the agent however here's how it actually works: 1% goes to Broker, 1% is used for professional photography and to market the property and then 1% goes to the agent, before they pay taxes, now,

7. If an agent is going to discount their commission, do you believe the agent's Broker is going to get their money?

8. Do you believe the agent is going to get paid their portion to take home to their family?

9. What do you think will be left out with agents that discount?

10. This is why we see agents that discount their commission not able to market their listings and therefore the property takes longer to sell, which causes the property to sell for less money, so,

11. On the outside, it looks like having an agent that will discount their commission might be better but if you ended up getting 10%-12% less for your home than you could have gotten, would that be acceptable?

12. So let's do this, I feel 100% confident that I can get your home sold for a premium which will net you the money you need and if you're comfortable with me, let's go ahead and move forward and if there's ever a day that you feel different, you have the right to fire me at anytime, is that reasonable?

"WE WANT TO INTERVIEW OTHER AGENTS"

1. That makes sense,

2. And interviewing more than one agent is smart, so

3. Can I ask you, are you OK with the pricing strategy we talked about?

4. Great and the numbers we talked about with my flexible commission all makes sense and sounds fair?

5. Perfect and are you comfortable with me as your agent if we did decide to move forward?

6. OK got it, so you just want to make sure that before we commit to working together, you at least have some perspective of what another agent would have to say, is that right?

7. Makes total sense and so let's do this, if you want, we can go ahead get the paperwork completed now and if for some reason you meet with another agent and decide not to work with me, I'll personally come back, rip up the paperwork with you and we can shake hands and walk our separate way, fair enough?

"WE THINK OUR HOUSE IS WORTH MORE MONEY"

1. Absolutely,

2. And if I'm you, I want to make sure I don't leave any money on the table and get the most for my house as possible, which is what you want, right?

3. Totally makes sense, and so let's do this, we can enter the market at the price you feel confident with, and given that the average time it takes for homes like yours to sell is 17 days, one of three things will happen:

    a. We should anticipate tons of traffic and showings and an offer within the first two weeks.

    b. Or, we get a ton of traffic and showings, but no one writes an offer which means the buyers don't agree with our price, make sense?

    c. Lastly, if we hit the market and don't get any traffic, while all the homes around us are selling, this is the market's way of telling us the price is NOT in line and we'd need to adjust within the first two weeks to avoid becoming a stale listing, does that seem reasonable?

"WE WANT TO THINK IT OVER AND GET BACK TO YOU"

1. That makes sense,

2. Obviously, this is a big decision

3. Can I ask you, are you OK with the pricing strategy we talked about?

4. Great and the numbers we talked about with my flexible commission all makes sense and sounds fair?

5. Perfect and are you comfortable with me as your agent if we did decide to move forward?

6. OK got it so you just want to make sure that before we commit to working together, you at least have some time to think it through, is that right?

7. Makes total sense and so let's do this, if you want, we can go ahead get the paperwork completed now and if for some reason you decide not to work with me, I'll personally come back, rip up the paperwork with you and we can shake hands and walk our separate way, fair enough?

"WE WANT TO LIST WITH A FLAT FEE BROKER"

1. I totally understand,

2. And if I was you, listing with a flat fee broker to save money might make sense,

3. Can I share with you some red flags to consider when working with those companies?

4. Obviously, it looks appealing to work with those companies to get your house in the MLS for a low fee to get the home sold but netting the most money bottom line is the ultimate goal, right?

5. Right and are you familiar with their "List-to-Sold Price Ratio?"

6. Flat fee brokers only get about 75% of the seller's asking price on average vs. listing with full service brokerage, which gets about 97% depending on the agent, so

7. Let's do this, why don't we move forward together and if the day ever comes where you don't think I'm earning my commission, you can fire me and hire a flat fee broker anytime you want,

8. Is that fair?

REVERSE SELLING APPOINTMENT-SETTING SCRIPTS

TIP: These scripts use all six of the skills in the Reverse Selling hexagon. Listening, AARA, Removing Resistance, Gaining Agreement, Socratic Questioning, Reverse Close.

1. Let's not agree to anything over the phone, LET'S SIMPLY schedule time to meet and review a plan that will cause your home to sell and then after we've had a chance to meet, you can decide if working with me makes sense or not, fair enough?

2. *(Name)*, what I'd like to do, is stop by one day, take a look at the home and when I'm there, we can review a plan to get the home sold and then after we meet, you can decide if working with me as your agent makes sense or not, does that sound fair?

3. *((Name)*, obviously you're not going to do anything unless it makes sense, which is why maybe we can schedule time to meet one day this week, review a plan that will cause your home to sell and then after we've had a chance to meet, you can decide if working with me makes sense or not, does that sound reasonable?

4. At this point, I think it makes sense for us to schedule time to get together one day, I can take a look at your home, I'll give you an honest assessment of the value and what I would do to get you top dollar and after our meeting, you can simply decide if working with me is a good fit or not, does that sound fair?

REVERSE SELLING LISTING CONSULTATION SCRIPT

    Part 1 — Setting the Agenda

    Part 2 — Discovery

    Part 3 — CMA Presentation

    Part 4 — Value Proposition Presentation

    Part 5 — Net Sheet Presentation

    Part 6 — Plan of Action Presentation

    Part 7 — Reverse Close

Part 1 — Setting the Agenda

1. OK so there's really three things we'll go through today.

    a. How to get your home sold for the highest price and not only the highest price, but attract buyers to pay you more than what other homes in the area are selling for

    b. How we'll ensure that you NET the most money in your pocket bottom line

    c. After we go through my plan of action, we can discuss whether or not it makes sense for us to work together to get your home sold, does all that sound fair? (Reverse Trial Close)

2. Great, so I'd like to clarify something before we start, most agents will try and tell you what you want to hear and try to make things sound better than they are in hopes you'll list your home with them, I would prefer to be 100% upfront and honest so that we can have a great experience working together, would that be OK?

3. Perfect because I brought a list of homes that failed to sell because the agent

was scared to tell the seller the truth and I'm only interested in helping you to successfully get the home sold! Too many agents are only interested in getting their sign out front for recognition, I'd rather only work together if we both of the same goal of actually getting the home sold and getting successfully moved, would you agree?

4. OK perfect because it's my goal at this time that at the end of the process when we're sitting at the closing table together that you'll feel comfortable and confident to possibly introduce me to people in the future that may need to buy or sell which is how I measure whether or not you had a positive experience working with me, sound fair?

Part 2 — Discovery

5. So before we get started, I want to make sure I'm on the same page, can you share with me what has you wanting to move/sell?

6. Makes sense, and ideally, when would you like to be done with this process and be moved into your new home?

7. Got it, now just so I understand, is it an option to just stay here and not sell at all?

8. I see...and with all of the moving pieces to selling a home and making a big move, what would you say is your biggest concern right now?

9. (Paraphrase what you hard and move on to the next step)

Part 3 — CMA Pricing Presentation

10. So let's start off with understanding the market and creating your pricing strategy and to do so, the home must sell 3 times, can I explain? (Offer, Inspection, Appraisal)

11. So, in order for you to control the process instead of the buyer, we have to have a pricing strategy that gives you all the leverage, make sense?

12. So here's a snapshot of the local market so we can understand what we're up against. (Show Market Snapshot report)

13. So in order to ensure your home sells for a premium and you have the leverage in the negotiation process, it's all going to come down to how long it takes to generate an offer that we accept, I'll refer to this as Days on Market, here's how it works...

14. Homes that get offers immediately after hitting the market will always have a higher list-to-sold price ratio than homes that sit on the market for a long period of time and many times will get more than what they're asking for this reason...

15. If you're the buyer for this home and it's been on the market for 1 day with multiple buyers interested, what kind of offer would we need to present to the seller?

16. That's right! Because if the home you wanted was on the market for a long time, we'd be able to be more aggressive in our negotiations, that makes sense, right?

17. Now obviously, when we hit the market, you want to be the seller who gets an offer right away and has all the leverage, would you agree?

18. Perfect! The question then becomes how? It's simple, we need to be the obvious choice when we hit the market so buyers are attracted to your home like a magnet so let's jump into the analysis and I'll show you what I mean.

19. Price Bracketing — First, it's important that we understand the price bracketing strategy. When we get to the actual pricing, we need to position your home in the right bracket so that your home clearly stands out from the crowd as the obvious choice to potential buyers.

20. Here's an example: (Use a price range that does not reflect their price) Buyers search homes online in price brackets just like you and I. $200 to $250, $250 to $300, etc., which makes sense right?

21. A home that has a value range of $240,000 to $260,000 should be priced at $250,000, not $249,900 or $259,900, can you see why? (Explain the power of being in both brackets)

22. Active Listing Analysis — Homes for sale now act as our competition. Our goal is to use them to help us stand out. We do that by closely analyzing the features, benefits and price of each home for sale and how that might affect our pricing strategy. (Review with seller and how those homes compare)

23. Pending Listing Analysis — Homes that have accepted an offer will give us the best data because they tell us what buyers like and how much they are willing to spend RIGHT NOW. (Review with seller and how those homes compare)

24. Sold Listing Analysis — Homes that have sold in the past give us the facts and most likely the homes that will be used on your appraisal. We have to get the appraiser to agree. (Review with seller and how those homes compare)

25. Now based on the data, the market suggests the home should sell for somewhere between *X to X* and my recommendation is that we enter the market at *X* so that we are the obvious choice and have buyers competing for your home, does that make sense? (Only move on when a price has been agreed to)

Part 4 — Value Proposition Presentation

26. Now any time a seller looks at hiring an agent, I believe that the seller takes on a huge risk…why? Because they don't really know what they're getting and can only go off what the agent is saying…

27. So, I've designed a program to transfer the risk and accountability off of you as the seller and on to me to perform which is the way it should be, would you agree?

28. So if we thought it made sense to work together, the first thing is that I have a ONE DAY AGREEMENT.

29. It's very simple, as long as things are moving that way we both want, we keep moving forward but if there comes a time where you think I'm not holding up my end, you'll have the right to fire me, does that seem fair?

30. Great and it goes both ways. (Make a joke about you the agent having the same right if the seller turns out to be difficult)

31. So, the next thing is what I call the "Savvy Seller Agreement."

32. This gives you the right to bring a buyer to the table, is it likely, no, but if a friend, family member, or co-worker wants to buy your house,

33. I would act as the "Transaction Coordinator" and coordinate the contracts, addendums, disclosures, inspections, appraisal, title work and the closing and you'd only end up paying a 1% commission, make sense?

34. Perfect and lastly, that leads me right into my "Flexible Commission" structure,

35. We just discussed what happens if you bring a buyer but there's two other ways I'll generate the buyer,

36. The first is if through my own marketing efforts directly to buyers I find a buyer who does not have their own agent, you'd only end up paying a 4% commission and,

37. Lastly, through marketing to other agents, I get them to bring one of their buyers, we'd pay 3% to that agent's company and my company would get 3%, all that make sense?

38. Perfect, now going through all of that, are those terms something you're comfortable with and do they seem fair? (Reverse Trial Close)

Part 5 — Net Sheet Presentation
(we give three scenarios on price: high, most likely, and low)

39. So, let's break down the numbers so you can get a good idea of how much you'll net from the sale,

40. What we're looking at right now are three worst case scenarios as these numbers assume another agent brings the buyer and NO TAX PRORATIONS are included so,

41. There's really only three things a seller is responsible for, real estate costs, title and transfer tax, and the rest is the covered by the buyer

42. Now, transfer tax is always .876% of the sales price, which is this number here...

43. And the seller is responsible for providing an owner's title policy, which is about $400-$500 per $100K in sales price and that this number here

44. And this number represents the real estate costs

45. And here's what you can expect to walk away with in your pocket when this home sells, worst case scenario, (point to the most likely number), can you live with this? (Reverse Trial Close)

Part 6 — Plan of Action Presentation

46. Awesome, so let's walk through the process so you can understand what to expect as we move forward (Assumptive)
47. Everything starts with our professional photo shoot (Short explanation of the importance)
48. Now typically we get photos back and the listing is ready for you to review, 2 to 3 days after the shoot,
49. So when do you think you could have the house ready for photos? (Reverse Trial Close) (Write down date and time)
50. Now, once we get everything back, we'll send you the listing to review and approve
51. Once you approve the listing, I'll install the lockbox and the sign will get installed, so let's talk about how showing the home will work,
52. When there's a fully qualified buyer who wants to view your home, I can notify you a couple different ways, I can call you, text you or email you and then you can approve or decline that time, which would work best? (Reverse Trial Close)

Part 7 — Reverse Close

53. Does all this make sense so far?
54. Perfect! So, after talking with you, I feel 100% comfortable working with you and confident that I can sell your home, do you feel comfortable with me as your agent and are you ready to get started? (Be confident and ask for the business)
55. Perfect, well, let's go ahead and get some paperwork completed and then I can get to work, let's start with the seller disclosure statements.

www.reverseselling.com

Made in the USA
Las Vegas, NV
25 September 2021